WORD
BIBLICAL
THEMES

WORD
BIBLICAL
THEMES

Daniel

JOHN E. GOLDINGAY

WORD PUBLISHING
Dallas · London · Sydney · Singapore

DANIEL

Word Biblical Themes

Quotations from the Scriptures in this volume are the author's own translation unless otherwise indicated.

Library of Congress Cataloging-in-Publication Data

Goldingay, John.
    Daniel / John Goldingay.
        p.   cm. — (Word Biblical themes)
    Includes bibliographical references.
    ISBN 0-8499-0794-2
    1. Bible. O.T. Daniel—Theology. I. Title. II. Series.
BS1555.5.G72   1989
224′.506—dc20   89-38306
                                                              CIP

Printed in the United States of America
9 8 0 1 2 3 9 RRD 9 8 7 6 5 4 3 2 1

CONTENTS

Contents

FOREWORD

Finding the great themes of the books of the Bible is essential to the study of God's Word, and to the preaching and teaching of its truths. But these themes or ideas are often like precious gems; they lie beneath the surface and can only be discovered with some difficulty. The large commentaries are most useful to this discovery process, but they are not usually designed to help the student trace the important subjects within a given book of Scripture.

The *Word Biblical Themes* meet this need by bringing together, within a few pages, all of what is contained in a biblical volume on the subjects that are thought to be most significant to that volume. A companion series to the *Word Biblical Commentary*, these books seek to distill the theological essence of the biblical books as interpreted in the more technical series and to serve it up in ways that will enrich the preaching, teaching, worship, and discipleship of God's people.

Daniel is an exciting and meaningful narrative concerning Jews in exilic times followed by a series of visions which interpret God's actions affecting the Jews in the succeeding centuries. In this book, Dr. John Goldingay has condensed the insights gained from his work on Daniel in the *Word Biblical Commentary* and has presented them here for pastor and student and scholar.

This volume is sent forth in the hope that it will contribute to the vitality of God's people, renewed by the Word and the Spirit and ever in need of renewal.

Southern Baptist Theological
    Seminary
Louisville, Kentucky

John D. W. Watts
Old Testament Editor
Word Biblical Commentary
Word Biblical Themes

PREFACE

The Book of Daniel has been appreciated as children's stories. It has been studied as a key example of biblical apocalyptic. It has been read as a preview of events to unfold at Christ's second coming. But none of these interests in the book corresponds to its author's priorities. He was concerned to bring a message of encouragement and challenge to people who were under pressure—people in lands far from home (where the book affirms the possibility of faithfulness, protection, and even success at the pagan court), and people under pressure in their own country (where they are browbeaten towards apostasy by a foreign overlord, and need to be reassured that God really is in control of their destiny). It speaks of God's faithfulness, God's sovereignty, and God's insight, and the way God shares those with people. It offers a perspective on the history of the post-exilic period, on the crisis that overcame Jews in Jerusalem in the reign of Antiochus Epiphanes, and on the End God promised. It calls people to prayer and reminds them of how heaven is involved in their destinies.

I much appreciated the opportunity to contribute the volume on Daniel to the *Word Biblical Commentary*; I said everything I know about Daniel in the commentary, so there is virtually nothing here that does not appear in one form or another there, but I hope the form of this book makes the themes of Daniel accessible to another readership and draws them into deeper faith, surer hope, and steadier commitment before Daniel's God.

1   INTRODUCTION

Two very different features have attracted readers to the Book of Daniel. It opens with a series of dramatic stories relating the adventures of Daniel and three other men at the Babylonian and Persian court. The four distinguish themselves by their skill as counselors to a series of kings, in particular by their ability to interpret the dreams and other omens which come to the kings. They serve at court without compromising their commitment to the God of Israel. Indeed, they show themselves willing to accept martyrdom rather than go back on that commitment, while their God honors their faithfulness by seeing that they escape when martyrdom threatens.

The other feature of the book is a series of extraordinary dreams and other revelations given to Daniel himself, which dominate the second part of the book. To a large extent these visions are couched in code and symbol—beasts coming out of the sea, a ram and a goat doing battle, unnamed northern and southern kings seeking to conquer each other. Many features of the visions are thus puzzling to understand.

The straightforward division between stories and visions is complicated by some subtleties which emerge when we look at the chapters one by one. Daniel 1 is clearly an introduction. It tells how four young exiles gain wisdom and prestige without losing holiness, and thus sets the scene for the stories that follow by explaining how the exiles came to be in Babylon, in positions of responsibility and bearing Babylonian names, and how they maintained their faithfulness to their God from the beginning. Further, it sets the book as a whole in the context of the seventy years of exile which are covered by both stories and visions, throughout which Daniel functioned. It thus lays the foundation for a consideration of the question when Jeremiah's promise of Jerusalem's restoration will at last be fulfilled (see esp. Daniel 9).

Daniel 2 illustrates Daniel in particular exercising at court those consummate gifts of insight which the introduction has attributed to him, and proving that the God of Israel is the source of true discernment. But the story aspect to the chapter gives way in the second half to a concern with the actual content of God's revelation to Nebuchadnezzar. The revelation concerns the significance of Nebuchadnezzar's own reign and that of three other reigns to follow, the last of which will be supernaturally destroyed and replaced by God's own rule. As a story, Daniel 2 introduces further motifs which will reappear in the stories in Daniel 3–6. The dream-revelation also links with later material, especially Daniel 7, where the seer receives another revelation concerning the Babylonian empire and three subsequent empires, the last of which is followed by God's own rule.

There is thus a particular link between Daniel 2 and 7. There is also a connection between the stories in Daniel 3 and 6. In both, Judean exiles in positions of authority are put in a position where a royal edict requires them to contravene a fundamental requirement of their faith. In both, they are indicted by jealous colleagues, accused of treason, and sentenced to an unpleasant death. In both, the king rises in agitation to perceive that their God has sent a heavenly aide to deliver them. In both, the king orders others to be executed in their stead, and declares that all peoples are to recognize the power of their God.

Daniel 4 and 5 also link, though in a different way. They concern two successful kings of Babylon, father and son. One is an overbearing ruler who receives a portentous dream which his Babylonian advisers cannot interpret. Daniel, however, explains that it is God's warning regarding divine judgment to come. Judgment falls as God said, but the king in due course finds mercy. In the succeeding story, in which Daniel himself and the queen mother refer back to events narrated in the previous one, that king's sacrilegious son receives a portentous omen which his Babylonian advisers cannot interpret, the writing of an enigmatic message on the wall. Daniel, however, again explains that it is God's warning regarding divine judgment to come. Judgment falls as God said, but the king finds no mercy.

The further revelations that follow Daniel 7 relate back to it and also relate to each other. Daniel 8 explicitly looks back to the revelation in chapter 7, and some of the motifs in Daniel 7 reappear—notably a strange horn belonging to the last animal in the vision, small at first but growing very big and acting particularly aggressively. The structure of Daniel 8 parallels that of Daniel 7—a vision concerning a series of animals, and an interpretation that takes them as symbols of empires from Babylon onwards and promises God's ending of their oppression. The identity of the empires which will follow Babylon, about which Daniel 2 and 7 are rather allusive, is clear here: they are Media, Persia, and Greece (v 20). The rule of Greece comes to a climax with the second-century ruler of the Seleucid empire, Antiochus IV (Antiochus Epiphanes).

Daniel 9 takes up chapter 8's concern with "insight" and takes further its promise concerning the restoration of

3

desolate Jerusalem and its temple. It begins with a question concerning Jeremiah's prophecy of an end of the exile after seventy years, but its heart is a long prayer of Daniel's which arises out of that prophecy. If Daniel 9 has links with earlier material in the book, these are with Daniel 1 as much as with Daniel 8.

Daniel 10–12 is one revelation given special emphasis by its length and its location at the end of the book. The introductory vision (chapter 10) parallels the one in Daniel 8, but is on a larger scale. The actual account of events to come (chapter 11) offers the plainest and most clear-cut of the historical visions, explaining and decoding those of earlier chapters. The portrait of the End (chapter 12) works out some of its implications for people whom death seems to rob of the chance to share in them. The revelation as a whole links back with the stories by portraying Israel's leaders experiencing the same afflictions as are described in Daniel 1–6 and challenged to be as steadfast as the heroes of the stories were.

The book might thus be outlined as follows:

1. Exile and the questions it raises: story
   2. A vision of four empires
      3. A trial of faithfulness and a marvelous deliverance
         4. An omen interpreted and a king challenged and chastised
         5. An omen interpreted and a king challenged and deposed
      6. A trial of faithfulness and a marvelous deliverance
   7. A vision of four empires
   8. Aspects of this vision developed
9. Exile and the questions it raises: vision
10–12. Aspects of this vision developed

A number of further stories about Daniel and further visions attributed to him appear in the longer Greek version of the book (see e.g., the Jerusalem Bible) and in later collections of revelatory visions or "apocalypses."

The book's historical background

The stories of Daniel and his friends are thus set in the period of the Exile, in the sixth century B.C. But some aspects of the stories (e.g., the many Persian words they contain) suggest that in the form we know them the stories come from well into the Persian period, which lasted from the latter part of the sixth century to the latter part of the fourth. With the visions, matters are even more complicated. They include allusions to events long after Daniel's day. Insofar as these are events which take place in Old Testament times, they are especially ones that belong in the second century B.C., when the rule of Antiochus Epiphanes brought a great crisis to the covenant people. The Book of Daniel thus refers to known historical events over a period of nearly half a millennium, from the end of the seventh century to the middle of the second, and in understanding the book it is useful to have some overall idea of the history of the Jews over those centuries.

In 611 the Assyrian Empire with its center in the north of the area now known as Iraq fell before the renewed power of Babylon, in the south of Iraq, under King Nabopolassar (625–605). The people of Israel had been promised by prophets such as Nahum that the Assyrians would fall because of their inhumanity and pride. But the Babylonians were no better, as Habakkuk pointed out to God, and Israel was soon in rebellion against them and inclined to ally with the Egyptians in seeking to throw off Babylonian overlordship. For Babylon, Israel was a useful buffer state on the edge of their empire, and was a nuisance when it insisted on rebelling every time the Babylonians' backs were turned.

The two decades beginning in 605 thus saw a series of punitive expeditions to Israel by or on behalf of Nabopolossar's great son and successor, Nebuchadnezzar II (605–562), which came to a first climax with the sack of Jerusalem in 597. More than one of these expeditions led to the taking back to Babylon of hostages from the royalty and the nobility in Jerusalem as a way of depriving the city of the leadership to encourage further revolt, and these acts are the background for the story of the displacement of Daniel and his three friends, among others, in Daniel 1.

After Nebuchadnezzar's long reign his immediate successors (Evil-Merodach, 562–560; Neriglissar, 560–556; and Labashi–Marduk, for a few months in 556) reigned for only a short time and made little impression on the Old Testament writers. The last Babylonian king, Nabonidus, reigned from 556 until the empire's defeat by the Persians in 539. He also lacks direct mention in the Old Testament, though he lies behind the surface at a number of points, not least in Daniel. For most of his reign he abandoned the city of Babylon itself and moved his headquarters to Tema towards the north-western end of his empire. The reasons for this are a matter of dispute; the move may have had a good political or religious rationale, though it was portrayed by his enemies within Babylon as the act of a madman.

Nabonidus's dedication of an image of the god Sin and his withdrawal to Tema have been seen as underlying the stories of Nebuchadnezzar building an image in Daniel 3 and going into exile in the wild in Daniel 4. The interest which the Nebuchadnezzar of Daniel shows in dreams also parallels more closely what we know from elsewhere of Nabonidus than what we know of Nebuchadnezzar. Less disputedly, Nabonidus lies behind Daniel 5, since Belshazzar was none other than Nabonidus's son and regent during his stay in Tema. Though Nabonidus returned east as the Persians advanced on Babylon, it was Belshazzar who effectively ruled there for the last decade of the empire's life.

Babylon was actually taken and briefly ruled on behalf of the Persians by a general called Gobryas. In Daniel 6, the first post-Babylonian ruler of Babylon is one Darius the Mede. He is a puzzle, there being no reference to him outside Daniel within the Old Testament or elsewhere. If we are to identify him with any otherwise known historical figure, it must probably be Gobryas. But the new emperor of Babylon, the first Lord of the enlarged Persian Empire, was Cyrus, who has already been mentioned at 1:21 and now appears at 6:28.

The Persians ruled the middle east for two centuries. "Three . . . then a fourth" subsequent Persian rulers are alluded to in Daniel 11:2. The expression is probably a figure of speech, as in Proverbs 30 and Amos 1-2, and the allusion may cover the sequence of Persian rulers as a whole, though it may have in mind the three or four who are mentioned in the Old Testament. After Cyrus these rulers (and their approximate dates) were Cambyses (530-522), Smerdis (522), Darius I (522-486), Xerxes I (486-465), Artaxerxes I (465-424), Xerxes II (424), Sogdianos (424-423), Darius II (423-405), Artaxerxes II (405-359), Artaxerxes III (359-338), Artaxerxes IV (338-336), and Darius III (336-30).

In 336 Alexander the Great became ruler of Macedon and in 333 invaded the Middle East, defeating the Persians and creating an empire that stretched from present-dayTurkey to India. Daniel 11 outlines the history of the next two centuries from a Palestinian perspective, concentrating on the reigns of Antiochus III and IV, especially the latter.

Alexander himself died less than a decade after crossing into Asia. His empire was nominally controlled for some years by members of his family, but its real rulers were Alexander's former generals who had controlled the satrapies into which the empire was divided. Four major units eventually emerged from his shattered realm, though two were more powerful than the others. One was that focused on Egypt and ruled by Alexander's general Ptolemy and his successors. The other was that focused on Syria and Babylonia and ruled by another general, Seleucus (once satrap of Babylonia and then one of Ptolemy's generals: see Daniel 11:5), and his successors. These two realms lying either side of Palestine were the ones that directly concerned Judea, which constituted a bone of contention between them, as it had between earlier powers. The story in Daniel 11 thus relates substantially to relationships between these "northern" and "southern" kings.

About 250, Ptolemy attempted to improve relations with the Seleucid empire by marrying his daughter to Antiochus II, but the plan failed when Antiochus's former wife took her revenge on the parties involved, provoking an Egyptian invasion of Syria (11:6–9). In the last decades of the century Antiochus III (223–187) in turn set about making war in the south, recapturing lost territory and in due course winning a key battle against the Egyptian army in Palestine at Banias (Caesarea Philippi) in 199. This enabled him to annex Palestine, though not to fulfill further ambitions on the Egyptian empire, which were thwarted by the feared and then by the actual intervention of Rome in the Middle East, and finally by Antiochus III's own assassination (11:10–19).

Seleucus IV (187–175), remembered for his attempted pillage of the Jerusalem temple treasury (11:20), was succeeded by Antiochus IV (175–164)—Seleucus's brother, but not the heir apparent (11:21–45). In Jerusalem he won the support of the Tobiad family, a group willing to cooperate with Antiochus in order to win power there, and not too concerned about detailed observance of the Law of Moses. Antiochus replaced the high priest, Onias III, who by his office carried authority in both religious and secular affairs, by his brother Jason, an ally of the Tobiads. The Seleucid army then invaded Egypt and won spectacular but not conclusive victories; Antiochus's designs there were finally frustrated by further Roman intervention ordering Antiochus off Egyptian territory.

On two occasions in the course of his campaigns he also took action against Jerusalem, both to augment his financial resources from those of the temple and to put down a rebellion on the part of conservative Jews against the Tobiad ruling party supported by Antiochus. The king then stationed a Syrian garrison in Jerusalem against the possibility of further rebellion, but this involved also introducing the worship of the garrison's Syrian gods. Perhaps as a result of a further act of rebellion at that provocation, in due course orthodox Jewish worship was proscribed. Nominally conservative Jews then had to choose between apostasy and resistance. Courageous active rebellion saw the temple worship restored and Antiochus withdraw from Judea; he was assassinated at the end of 164.

The book's origin

The summaries we have given above indicate the striking double focus of the Book of Daniel. The stories center on Jews who lived in the sixth century and on issues that were important for people in the dispersion. The revelations, however, wherever we can be sure of the situation to which they relate, speak to the predicament of Jews who lived in Jerusalem in the second century in the religious crisis brought about in Judea by the political policies of Antiochus IV.

So was the book written in the sixth century or in the second (or some time in between)? Was it that God led sixth-century believers to put into writing stories that directly spoke to issues that concerned their situation in exile, and also gave them previews of events to unfold over the next four centuries which would be primarily relevant to Jerusalem in the second century? Or was it that God led second-century believers to collect earlier stories of the

9

faithfulness which Jews experienced from God and showed to God, and gave them further revelations regarding their destiny now, which built on that earlier material and which they could add to it?

In discussing this question scholars have taken into account a number of factors such as the nature of the languages in which Daniel is written (a mixture of Hebrew and Aramaic with a number of words imported from Persian, Greek, and other languages). But the most significant determinant of their attitudes has been their attitude to that fundamental question of what God seems more likely to have done.

In my opinion the second view is much the more likely; see further the discussion of the visions in the book at the end of chapter 4 below. But one's attitude to this question makes no necessary difference to one's understanding of the contents of the book, so that readers who take the traditional view that the book was written in the sixth century will not necessarily thereby find that they disagree about the book's themes.

2 FAITHFULNESS—DIVINE AND HUMAN

Daniel begins with a strange event: the God of Israel gives over to a cruel foreign power both Israel's king and Jerusalem, with the temple and its effects. Yahweh had entered into commitment in perpetuity to David and his descendants and to Zion and its shrine (see e.g., Ps 132). What has happened to the faithfulness of God?

Other Old Testament books have a clear answer to that question. Jerusalem and its monarchy fell because the people and the kings persistently resisted God's will. God had entered into a covenant relationship with them, but that covenant required a response on their part. In the absence of that response, the relationship collapsed. The fall of Jerusalem is a sign of that. Daniel's prayer in Daniel 9 shows that Daniel accepts that assessment of Israel's position, but this makes it all the more striking that such an explanation of God's strange behavior is missing here.

It may be that the story omits to note that the Exile came about through Israel's disobedience to God because this was not directly relevant to the circumstances of the later generations for whom the book was written. By the time of Daniel's later years most Jews in Babylon will have been people who were born there; they were victims of the Exile rather than responsible for it. Nor do the visions see the residents of Jerusalem in the second century as personally responsible for the affliction that comes to them; they are victims despite the fact that very many of them shared a desire to shape their lives by God's word. The experience of being in exile and the experience of being oppressed in their own land thus raised questions about the faithfulness of God.

These experiences also raise questions about the faithfulness of God's people. Circumstantial evidence suggests that being taken into exile put pressure on distinctive Jewish practices such as observance of the sabbath, adherence to the food laws, and the rite of circumcision; it is these that Genesis emphasizes as it tells the story of creation, flood, and God's covenant with Abraham. In the stories in Daniel, the stress is on commitment to purity (Dan 1), avoidance of idolatry (Dan 3), and insistence on prayer (Dan 6). In the visions, the underlying theme is the challenge to maintain faithful worship when Antiochus pressures the people into apostasy. At such points Israelites are put on the spot with regard to their faithfulness to God and forced to face the question of whether they will maintain their commitment, trusting that as they do so God will be faithful to them.

Faithfulness in lifestyle

The issue arises first in connection with food. When they are taken into exile, as former members of the Israelite royal family, Daniel, Hananiah, Mishael, and Azariah are also introduced to the Babylonian court. As well as learning the Babylonian language, acquiring skill in Babylonian wisdom, and accepting Babylonian names, they are naturally expected to share the food and wine of the court. Daniel, on behalf of all four, demurs. It would be something that would "defile" them (1:8).

What precisely would be defiling about it is not explicit. Christians have often felt uneasy about the food laws in the Bible and have suspected that the Book of Daniel is here falling into the external legalism of which Christians are inclined to suspect Jews. It may be doubted whether the Bible's food laws ever need be an expression of legalism; and anyway the reference to "wine" does not fit the suggestion that the background to the passage is the specific laws about food in Leviticus and Deuteronomy. Daniel's attitude need not imply that there was anything inherently wrong about the food the Babylonians ate (e.g., that it was unhealthy or gained by unethical means or had been offered to a Babylonian god).

The idea of defilement presupposes that there are objects or activities that are quite in place for some people but not for others. There was food ordinary Israelites could eat which priests could not, and that helped to give outward expression to the difference between priests and people and helped to keep them separate. There was food foreigners could eat which Israelites could not, and that helped to mark the difference in God's purpose between Israel and the nations and helped to prevent Israel's being swallowed up among the gentile peoples. All this reflects the fact that what we eat and drink, like what we wear and how we speak, is often an outward expression of our self-identity and our commitments; we preserve these differences in order to preserve ourselves. Although in Christ such differences between priests and people and between Israel and the world would be abolished, before Christ it was important that they be preserved.

Preserving differences in this way is particularly important for people in exile or under persecution. Indeed, exile was an inherently defiling experience (cf. Isa 52:11; Hos 9:3, 4; Amos 7:17). It threatened the separate distinctiveness of Israel. For Daniel and his friends pagan food and drink epitomize the pagan uncleanness they associated with exile in a foreign land. So Daniel's desire for abstinence symbolizes his avoiding assimilation, his being faithful to the God of Israel.

God's own faithfulness manifests itself first in the fundamentally sympathetic reception Daniel receives from the official in charge of the exiles. But how can he translate sympathy into action? He would be risking his own head if he allowed Daniel and his friends a diet which turned good-looking young men into skeletons. At this point Daniel's trust in God allows him to propose an astonishing wager, that ten days on a vegetarian diet (which would not seem as defiling as the king's meat and wine) would leave them looking healthier than anyone. What gave Daniel the idea we are not told: it is out of his mouth before there can be talk of thinking it through or seeking God's guidance. (See *Jerome's Commentary on Daniel* on this passage.) Daniel's words are a challenge to God as much as a gesture of trust in God. It is a challenge which God honors.

There is a further hint of the faithfulness of God in the closing observation, that Daniel remained in Babylon until the reign of King Cyrus. The chapter's opening note had raised implicit questions about the faithfulness of a God who could let his people be taken into exile. Its closing note does not quite answer that question (it does not say why he did so), but it does imply his caring providence in looking after Daniel and enabling him to outlast not merely the great Babylonian king of verse 1 but his entire empire!

The experience of exile and affliction raises classic questions about the sovereignty and the faithfulness of God. Daniel thus begins with a powerful declaration of faith in a God whose will can be accepted even when exercised in a strange way. God has allowed, indeed initiated, a terrible experience for Israel, but God is in control and can be trusted; somehow all must make sense.

Faithfulness in religious observance (Daniel 3)

The faithfulness of God and the faithfulness of exiled Israel come into focus again in the story of the three young men who choose burning rather than apostasy. In the Dispersion the testing of faithfulness in the fire took place literally for a few people, but also metaphorically for many others. The Exile itself is a white-hot crucible that threatens to consume Israel. Will they be faithful?

Nebuchadnezzar erects a gigantic golden image—perhaps of himself, more likely of a god he worships—to be dedicated in the presence of an impressive gathering of state dignitaries. Any who would not prostrate themselves before the statue would be burnt to death. But a Jew could not so bow down before an image; that would contravene a fundamental aspect of commitment to Yahweh.

For most Jews there was no problem here, because ordinary people were not required to attend this ceremony. The people for whom it was a problem were those who had attained positions of responsibility in the state, who would then have to discern where lay the limits to their acceptance of the state's authority. An impressive ceremony of this kind, reinforced by the sanction attached to neglecting it, embodies the double pressure of the pagan state—its attractiveness and its unscrupulousness.[1]

The story takes for granted the faithfulness of the three men at this point. There was no question of their taking part. The crisis arose for them as a result of another experience which became a familiar one for Jews in dispersion. Members of the host nation become jealous at their success. They inform the king of the action of the three, which he can see as disloyalty to him and to the state, and as impiety.

On all counts the penalty is that they must be burnt to death: "then whoever is the god who could rescue you from my power?" the king asks (3:15).

Faithfulness to and trust in God find remarkable expression in the three men's reaction to the king's terrible challenge. First, they say they do not actually need to make any response regarding what the king has said (3:16). They trust God to let events themselves determine the answer to the king's blasphemous rhetorical question.

But then they allow themselves one observation and one declaration of intent. If their God exists, they say, then this God is quite able to rescue them from Nebuchadnezzar's blazing hot furnace (3:17). It may seem odd for them to be treating the reality of their God as hypothetical (and because that seems odd, translators have often sought some alternative way of understanding their words). But Nebuchadnezzar has treated their God's existence as hypothetical, so they do the same for the sake of argument. For themselves, they have no doubt that God exists and that he can and will rescue them. Their confidence is the same as that Daniel showed when he made his wager over the vegetarian diet.

Their declaration of intent is that even if God should not rescue them, they will still remain faithful to their commitment (v 18). Again the translations vary, and the men have been thought to be saying that they will still maintain their stance even if God cannot rescue them or even if God does not exist, but that idea seems impossibly modern. Once more they are granting a theoretical possibility, that their God might not intervene, and assuring the hearers of this story that even this would make no difference to their stance. They are not faithful only because God is faithful to them, the accusation the Adversary threw at Job. Nor are they faithful to death knowing that they will enjoy resurrection—that possibility is unmentioned. They are faithful just for the sake of the rightness of their confession.

As in Daniel 1 God manifests a faithfulness which responds to theirs. Isaiah 43 promises God's own presence when Israel walks through the fire of exile. Here the divine aide who camps round those who honor God and delivers them from peril (Ps 34:7) enters the very fire to rescue them. Blasphemy is replaced by blessing, confrontation by recognition, opposition and persecution by tolerance and protection.

Faithfulness in prayer

In a later story Daniel, too, falls foul of the jealousy of his colleagues; here in Daniel 6, however, ordinary events fail to provide his political enemies with a means of bringing about his downfall, and they have to devise their own. Significantly, Daniel's vulnerability lies in his religious commitment, as was the case with the other three men. So his enemies contrive to ban prayer. His response to the prohibition on prayer is to continue praying. There is no fuss or rush about it, such as characterizes every action of his assailants. Nor is there any attempt to hide what he is doing: when prayer is fashionable, it is time to pray in secret (Matt 6:5, 6), but when prayer is under attack, it is important to make clear that one renders to God the things that are God's. Prayer seems an innocuous act, but here, at least, it was "more . . . revolutionary than outright rebellion would have been. Rebellion simply acknowledges the absoluteness and ultimacy of the emperor's power, and attempts to seize it. Prayer denies that ultimacy altogether by acknowledging a higher power."[2]

So Daniel is caught petitioning God when he is only allowed to petition the king, and is denounced. As was the case with the three men in Daniel 3, the accusation includes reference to his Jewish origin (6:13); the implication may be merely that a foreigner cannot be trusted to be loyal to the country in which he dwells, but there is a hint of anti-Semitism about the words. In contrast to the earlier story, we learn nothing of Daniel's words or feelings as he approaches execution; here the king himself says all that needs to be said about the possibility of Daniel's escape (6:16). "In testing Daniel, the king knows . . . that he is testing God."[3]

Just as the fact of God's faithfulness did not ensure that Daniel's friends would be preserved from the furnace, neither does it mean that Daniel will be preserved from the lion pit. It does lead to God's aide being sent into the furnace to stand with Daniel's friends, and also to God's aide being sent into the pit to stand with Daniel, so that as they were preserved in the furnace, so is he in the pit, "because he had trusted in his God" (6:23).

Faithfulness in worship

Four centuries later, Jews in Jerusalem came under pressures that were sufficiently similar to those experienced by Daniel and his three friends for their stories to be an inspiration and a challenge once more. The people of God are again tested "by sword [cf. 2:6, 12, 13] and by fire [cf. Daniel 3], by captivity [cf. Daniel 1] and by becoming prey [cf. Daniel 6]" (11:33).

Antiochus Epiphanes abolishes the daily sacrifices required by the Law of Moses and makes worship of his garrison's foreign gods the regular and mandatory worship of the temple (11:31). He is enabled to do this by the support of Jews who in the eyes of the orthodox have abandoned the covenant (11:30). Originally, perhaps, in their own eyes they had only been treating as insignificant some rather marginal requirements of the Torah; they had not seen themselves as being unfaithful to Yahweh. But as events have moved on, so have the pressures on Antiochus, and so have the pressures he thus places on the Tobiads. They are drawn into cooperation with a decision to abolish the distinctive practices of the Jewish religion. Antiochus thus "turns into apostates" people who had indeed "acted wickedly in relation to a covenant" (the term may refer to the covenant people whose oppression the Tobiads have already facilitated) (11:32). They still nominally maintain their Jewish faith but by their actions now they quite belie it. So what are other Jews to do?

Over against the people who have abandoned their faith, Daniel's vision puts "the people that acknowledges its God" (11:32). The passage uses the ordinary Hebrew word for "to know," which has the same range of meanings as the English word—to know facts, to know how to do something, to know a human being in a deeply personal way. In the prophets and elsewhere it is also used to mean "to acknowledge, to recognize, to commit oneself to": that is, it denotes a knowing that involves the will as well as the mind and feelings. "To know the law" or "to know the Lord" is a matter of obedience as well as acquaintance. That meaning fits well here.

Over against people whose knowledge of God and the Torah did not extend to obeying it, the vision sets a people whose knowledge includes a commitment of the whole person. The Hebrew term for these people who are truly committed to God is *hasidim* (cf. 1 Macc 2:42), a word still used today for people especially committed to obedience to the Torah. Their commitment or faithfulness expresses itself in offering "firm resistance" to Antiochus, which presumably included active attempts to prevent the implementing of his edict to abolish the worship required by the Torah and to replace it with pagan worship (see 1 Maccabees 1, 2). Since Daniel's vision describes how the community's "discerning ones will enlighten the multitude" (11:33), it seems that the *hasidim*, the committed ones, who resisted Antiochus, actually comprised the body of the Jewish community. Only the ruling party, the Tobiads, and people associated with them, accepted the edict. Hence many ordinary people went through the experiences described in Daniel 11:33.

Faithfulness—Divine and Human

Their faithfulness emulated that of Daniel and the other three men. However, their experience of God's faithfulness did not correspond to that of the four heroes.

Admittedly they did receive a "little help"—the reference most likely being to the successes of the first Judean activists (cf. 1 Macc 2–4), a real encouragement from God (though not something to be compared with the moment of ultimate victory, deliverance, awakening, and exaltation for whose coming they had to wait). It may have been those victories that drew into the resistance movement some people whose commitment could not be trusted in the long run (11:34). Perhaps it was the death of some of the leaders of the movement that exposed that. Now everything has to await the end which will come at the set moment (11:35). And in due course Antiochus indeed had to abandon his attempt to proscribe the Jewish faith.

But this came too late for many of Antiochus's victims. What does God's faithfulness mean for them? It is all very well for earlier chapters of the book to tell stories about God rescuing people from the fire and the lion pit, but more often the fire and the lions have devoured the martyrs. The stories in Daniel affirm that occasional experiences of the faithful God intervening on Israel's behalf are more important than the regular experience of God's nonintervention.

Not that we are expected to manifest a heroism that cares nothing for our own destiny. The visions in Daniel, and particularly chapters 10–12, encourage us to look for deliverance after death if not before it; and Christ's resurrection is for us the guarantee that such a deliverance is not mere fanciful hope. "It was the same God of the three youths who was the God of the Maccabees. The former escaped fire, the latter were executed by fires; but both will conquer in the eternal God."[4]

3 SOVEREIGNTY—DIVINE AND HUMAN

One of the characteristic convictions running through much of the Old Testament is the belief that God is sovereign in the history of Israel and in world events as they unfold, that God is working out a purpose for Israel and for the world in these events, and thus that history is the arena in which the person and the purpose of God are made known. Admittedly the pervasiveness of this theme in the Old Testament and the distinctiveness of Israel's belief in this activity of God in history have been exaggerated: there are parts of the Old Testament where it is unmentioned, and the peoples around Israel also believed that their gods controlled their historical destinies. But when we have made allowance for the exaggerations, it remains a characteristic Old Testament conviction that Yahweh is sovereign in history. It is a particularly important motif in the Book of Daniel, though one that raises many questions. Both in the Exile and in the second century, Israel goes through experiences that seem to belie belief in a God who controls history.

Related to the motif of the sovereignty of God is the motif of human sovereignty. The stories and the visions in Daniel concern how human kingship is exercised by Nebuchadnezzar and succeeding Babylonian and Persian rulers, and by successive Hellenistic monarchs leading up to Antiochus Epiphanes. They also concern how human kingship and divine kingship interrelate, and how people work out their political responsibilities to earthly kings without compromising their religious responsibilities to the heavenly king. How does one render to Caesar and also render to God?

The sovereignty of God and the Exile

As we noted in chapter 2, the Book of Daniel begins with an event which rings strange for people who believe that their God is sovereign in history: the king of Babylon attacks Jerusalem and takes it, carrying off to Babylon its king and some of the effects from the temple. It might seem to imply that Yahweh is no longer in control of Israel's history. On the contrary, the book affirms, this very event is a strange act on the part of their own God. It is God who gives over to a cruel foreign power both the king and the city, with its temple and its effects. The book does not indicate how Israel is to understand these events, but it does affirm that God's sovereignty is being worked out in them.

Daniel thus begins with a powerful declaration of faith in the sovereignty of God. He is in control, so somehow all must make sense. The end of the opening chapter of the book, as we noted, then returns to these questions, even if not quite to answer them. It draws attention to the fact that when Cyrus succeeds to the throne of this empire, Daniel is still there, enabled by God to outlast not merely the great

Babylonian king of verse 1 but his entire empire. God is sovereign in Israel's history, even when things look otherwise.

The God of heaven who changes times and eras

At the heart of Daniel 2 is a declaration of praise of God as sovereign in history and in the affairs of the nations. But the chapter begins with a portrait of a human sovereign—a rather negative portrait. Disturbed by a half-remembered dream, Nebuchadnezzar the man of brilliance, achievement, vision, and generosity, appears as mistrustful, angry, arbitrary, and violent. The account is cartoonlike, yet consistent with the portrayals of Middle Eastern courtly life in works such as Esther, the *Histories* of Herodotus, and *The Thousand and One Nights*.

The story illustrates the ambiguous prospects which attach to involvement in the Babylonian court. As in political life in the modern world, the power and glory of participation in the affairs of state would be attractive and an object of wistful longing for people who were not part of the secular power structure, which in that context would include Jews in general. At the same time, Babylonian court life would be alien and frightening because of its reputation for contention, betrayal, scandal, humiliation, and moral pressure. These motifs recur in the Daniel stories.

It is Daniel's search for God's revelation concerning Nebuchadnezzar's dream that leads him into praise when he receives his revelation from God (2:19-23). In the midst of this praise comes an abstract and systematic statement of the sovereignty of the God of heaven who is the God of the fathers. This God "changes times and eras" (2:21), the successive epochs ruled by one king or another, one empire or another. God indeed controls history. "He removes kings and establishes kings" (2:21). Daniel denies that history is determined by the planetary forces that the Babylonians studied (cf. Isa 40:25, 26). It is under God's direction.

This is not to imply that it is fixed by God irrespective of the process of human decision-making. Daniel has often been regarded as an example (*the* Old Testament example) of apocalyptic thinking, in the sense of speaking in terms of final events fixed since the beginning of time, of the whole world being under the power of evil, of a dualism of this wicked world and the righteous world to come, of judgment in the form of an immutable fate, and of a division of world history into periods predetermined by God.[1] But if this is apocalyptic thinking, Daniel is not apocalyptic. Like the authors of the Old Testament histories, Daniel assumes that human beings make real decisions which do shape history, yet that human decision-making does not necessarily have the last word in history. Daniel affirms the sovereignty of God in history, sometimes working via the process of human decision-making, sometimes working despite it.

As we have already noted, the Old Testament characteristically believes that Yahweh controls history, but elsewhere that conviction is generally expressed in connection with specific historical events (such as the victories of Cyrus over Babylon, in Isaiah 41). It is expressed here with a universality that is unusual. Daniel's testimony extends to God's control of history as a whole. The dream which Daniel explains does not relate just to a chapter in a man's life or a moment in an empire's history. It offers a perspective on the future as a whole. It was the God of Israel who gave Nebuchadnezzar not only Jerusalem (1:2) but all his royal might and power (2:37), indeed gave him authority over all creation (2:38). The world rulers are under God's control, and when God chooses they can be made to acknowledge it.

Furthermore, and paradoxically, Daniel's revelation—which speaks of God ruling in the future—actually effects the rule of God now. Nebuchadnezzar acknowledges that God already rules, "on earth as in heaven," and by giving God's servants authority over the sages and over Babylonian political affairs he institutes another indirect form of divine rule in Babylon itself, "on earth as in heaven." The fact that there is to be a new future, an End, does not mean we cannot hope for a new present—it makes a new present possible.

When readers of the Book of Daniel, who have seen regimes passing just as Daniel described, join Nebuchadnezzar in acknowledging that God is Lord of history, they make that acknowledgment with even greater conviction. God *is* Lord of history, whether or not we can see the evidence of that in history at the moment. History *is* going somewhere, even if that can only be perceived by divine revelation and not read off from the events themselves.

Sovereignty at work in the midst of history (i)

Nebuchadnezzar's dream in Daniel 2 portrays God's sovereignty at work on a grand scale as regime succeeds regime; its uncomfortable message comes home only for a successor several generations to come. Nebuchadnezzar's later dream (Dan 4) brings it home to Nebuchadnezzar in person.

The chapter begins with a declaration by this king who is the embodiment of sovereignty on earth. But he uses his authority to testify to the sovereignty of "God Most High," a description which appears more times here than in any other chapter in the Old Testament (4:2, 17, 24, 25, 32, 34). It is an expression at home on the lips of a pagan or an Israelite; to both it suggests a God of universal authority.

Daniel 4 also uses the word "heaven" more often than any other chapter, sometimes as a periphrasis for God or in the phrase "King of heaven" (4:26, 37), but more commonly to refer to the sky or to the place of God's dwelling, set over against the earth as the sphere of Nebuchadnezzar's rule and as the extent of his humiliation. Daniel 4 is centrally concerned with the kingship or sovereignty of Nebuchadnezzar and the kingship or sovereignty of the Most High God, the King of heaven, but from the beginning it makes clear the contrast between the sovereignty of one who rules on earth for a time and that of one who rules also in heaven and whose rule is unconstrained by time. His testimony will subvert any tendency to be overimpressed by the significance of mere human government.[2]

Nebuchadnezzar is a flourishing monarch and his dream concerns a flourishing, lofty, preeminent, verdant, protective, fruitful, long-lived tree—a common symbol for whatever is seen as ultimately alive, transcendent, life-giving, and sustaining. It is a natural symbol for a king such as Nebuchadnezzar, who mediates God's life, provision, and protection to his people. He is treelike to them, the embodiment of life and destiny, as presidents and prime ministers can still seem to be in our world. To a degree, Daniel affirms this significance of leaders, in that he challenges Nebuchadnezzar to do justice and to take action on behalf of the needy (4:27). It is by the observing of such priorities that leaders prove themselves treelike to their peoples.

When Daniel describes Nebuchadnezzar's achievements he does not imply that the king has fulfilled this royal ideal, and when Nebuchadnezzar speaks of his achievements, it is his (justifiable) pride in his building projects that he expresses, rather than his achievements in the area of justice and mercy. A great national empire such as Nebuchadnezzar's is the political equivalent of the Indian god Vishnu, who was supposed to be the Preserver of human life but whose huge image was traditionally carried in processions on a great wheeled throne that crushed anything that got in its path. The juggernaut which is supposed to be the preserver and provider easily becomes the crusher and the destroyer, totalitarian and absolute in its demands.[3]

It is apparently as much because of the exaggerated significance that comes to be attached to leaders as because of their specific failures that they have to fall, lest it seem that in truth all things hold together in anyone other than God. The tree is to be felled, so that people may acknowledge the sovereignty of the Most High over human sovereignty, not merely in the world above or in the age to come but in this world and in this age (4:14). Sometimes God exercises this rule *through* earthly kings, but sometimes *over* human kingship, demonstrating the power to deprive the mighty of their authority and to give it to "nobodies."

The tree is not, after all, a secure source of life and provision, and the felling of it will prove who is king. The one it symbolizes is to be reduced to an animal-like existence, living in the open, tethered to a metal ring, living off natural vegetation, exposed to the elements, his hair and nails growing wild. Reversal comes when Nebuchadnezzar looks to heaven (4:34), a phrase which suggests seeking God's aid and thus implicitly recognizing that *God* is king—as Nebuchadnezzar does explicitly once more at the chapter's close (4:37). His own rule can be suspended or terminated; God's cannot.

When Daniel first interprets the king's dream to him, there is no hint of his rejoicing in the disaster that hangs over the king. Daniel encourages us to long for God to have compassion on world rulers, specifically the wicked ones, and he encourages the world to believe that judgment is never inevitable. We are to treat people in power as given their responsibility by God. We are to appeal to their humanness, not to bait their sinfulness. The confession of God as king might seem to leave no place for human government. Actually the chapter assumes that if God's kingship is acknowledged, human sovereignty can then find its place. At the end of the story, even the majesty and glory of human kingship are affirmed. Rule on earth as well as the rule of heaven come to belong to the one who is poor in spirit.[4]

Sovereignty at work in the midst of history (ii)

Belshazzar's story begins like Nebuchadnezzar's, with a flourishing monarchy in royal majesty (5:1). But from the royal banquet issue sacrilege and blasphemy (5:2–4). The Exile might be thought to have established the power of the gods of Babylon over the God of Israel, and Belshazzar implicitly asserts the authority of Babylon and its gods over the exiles and their God. That provokes the latter to prove that the God who is treated as powerless has power and to expose the powerless Babylonian gods for what they are.

In interpreting the portent which Belshazzar has been given, Daniel begins by recalling the sovereign position that Belshazzar's "father" Nebuchadnezzar occupied (5:18–20). He possessed royal authority and splendor, the power of life and death, of ennoblement and disgrace. These are the kind of affirmations the Bible elsewhere makes of God, and Daniel begins by reminding Belshazzar that Nebuchadnezzar possessed them only as the gift of God. All human authority and power are an echo and a servant of that divine authority and power from which they derive and on which they depend.[5] But Nebuchadnezzar's power had become his weakness and had to be taken away. And Belshazzar has failed to learn the lesson, manifesting the same pride in the presence of the very Lord of heaven (5:23). Each of the two elements in this unique title for God, "Lord" and "heaven," suggest the almightiness of the One Belshazzar disdains.

On the surface the writing on the wall records the assessment of something in terms of monetary weights, "counted at a mina, a shekel, and two halves." But the three nouns also suggest three verbal roots, as in English "pounds" and "halves" can be verbs as well as nouns. Understood as verbs, "counted out," "weighed," and "broken in half," the words hint at three moments in God's dealings with Belshazzar as king. God appointed him; God is evaluating him in the present; God is imminently terminating his dynasty. Belshazzar is responsible to the heavenly sovereign for the way he has exercised his human sovereignty. God will now exercise the sovereignty of heaven in bringing about Belshazzar's fall.

Daniel's prophecy comes true with that common Middle Eastern phenomenon, a coup d'état. The heavenly sovereignty apparently operates via ordinary earthly means, though how this works out we are not told—only the sovereign purpose of God in the event is of interest. The end comes that very night, to make explicit that sovereign power of God and the authority of God's sage. The event illustrates how revolutionary violence can be an important factor through which God works in history; though what it brings in is not the final rule of God but the rule of Darius the Mede to replace that of Belshazzar the Chaldean.[6]

The worldly empire is demonstrated to be subject to the God of the Judean exiles. At the beginning of the story Belshazzar had flaunted the vessels captured from the temple in Jerusalem and encouraged the impression that Nebuchadnezzar was lord of history and that the God of Jerusalem was powerless, but the end of the story confounds that impression. Leaders may seem to be the embodiment of order, destiny, power, and divinity, but death comes to them, too, an incontrovertible denial of their pretension to ultimate power and significance.

Psalm 2 talks about God laughing when nations and governments assert themselves against him and his purpose. He knows they always end up falling into the pit they themselves dug. Hearing God's laughter is important for the Belshazzars of the world; it is a way God may get through to them.[7] It is

Sovereignty—Divine and Human

important for their subjects, too, who can afford to take them less seriously than they sometimes realize, and may be able to stand up to them better when they do realize it.

Human decrees and divine decrees

The state likes to have the support of religion, even if it formally keeps the two separate. The institution that claims absolute authority is inclined also to claim the sanctions of religion. Empires can have feet of clay and can fall apart, so it is as well for them to use all means to reinforce their strength and unity.[8] God is acknowledged not for God's sake, but because this helps to undergird the state.

The story in Daniel 3 describes an occasion when people were required to bow down before an image; the refusal of the three Israelites to do so is described first as contempt of the king's decree, only secondly as impiety (and even there as refusal "to serve *your* gods"). The personal nature of Nebuchadnezzar's rage suggests that the statue embodies not only a national and a religious commitment but also a personal one. Nebuchadnezzar's own standing was tied up with the statue. His expectation is, "You shall have no other god but me."[9] Can any *god* rescue the three men from *his* power? Events in due course provide him with his answer.

In the subsequent story in Daniel 6, Daniel himself ends up in the lion pit because a supposed human sovereignty allows itself to be used and manipulated in the name of its own authority. Daniel's jealous political colleagues engineer matters so that the law of Daniel's God (6:5) and the law of the Medes and Persians (6:8) are deliberately brought into conflict. As their means of putting Daniel out of the way they utilize the state's inclination to deify itself and the believer's obligation to confess no god but God. God's Law makes an absolute demand on human beings; so does the king's law, because he contributes to the state's stability and to the authority of his own position by insisting on the irrevocability of his injunctions. Once his decision is declared, it cannot be undone. Such firmness adds strength to good decisions, but compounds the weakness of poor ones. The law is the law is the law. If the king accepts it, he has to accept unacceptable constraints and unfairness when the law is an ass; if he suspends it, he risks the collapse of the social order, and ultimately of the state itself.[10]

Darius is unable to eat, relax, or sleep as he awaits the outcome of the action forced on him (6:18). When daylight comes, he returns to the lion pit in turmoil and trepidation instead of in the stately dignity and composure of a monarch. Daniel's "long live the king!" (6:22) strikingly affirms Darius's kingship, yet Darius's own acknowledgment of the living God either side of this greeting (6:20,26) relativizes this kingship of his. And that is what the event itself does—the stand Daniel takes, as much as the deliverance he experiences. One is reminded of stories from the early years of the church (Acts 4:18-20; 5:19, 20; 12:1-10; 16:19-26).

So "what happens when a state executes those who are praying for it?" They are "demonstrating the emperor's powerlessness to impose his will even by death. The final sanction had been publicly robbed of its power. Even as the lions lapped the blood of the saints, Caesar was stripped of his arms and led captive in Christ's triumphant procession. His authority was shown to be only penultimate after all."[11]

Daniel has obeyed God rather than the human sovereign, but has done no injury to the state (6:22). By putting loyalty to God above loyalty to the state he has been loyal to the truth, and thus more loyal to the state than those who make more of it than it is, and certainly than those who use it to serve their own ends. His story witnesses to the fact that heathen sovereignties do put believers under pressure, but that they are ultimately destined to bow before the name which is above every name. It is not merely a story about a miraculous escape from martyrdom, but about all human claims to sovereign immutability yielding to God's abiding will and about the miracle of the human sovereign himself acknowledging that.[12]

4 INSIGHT—DIVINE AND HUMAN

"Revelation" has been an important theme in the history of theology over recent centuries, and scholars have debated over the sense in which the Bible is God's revelation and over the way God is also revealed through creation or in history or through people's religious experience. The theme is not a prominent one in the Bible itself, but it runs throughout Daniel. Most of the stories note the insight of Daniel and the other young men, relate revelations given to them, and note the contrast between them and the Babylonian sages who cannot interpret portentous events which happen in their midst. They thus demonstrate that the God of Israel both possesses insight into history (as the One who is sovereign in history: see chapter 3) and shares it with the exiles. Each of the visions is a God-given unveiling of the mystery of history and serves as both a warning and a promise concerning its outcome.

Insight as God's gift

One of the first things we are told about the exiled young Jewish nobility among whom Daniel and his three friends are numbered is that they are "discerning in all aspects of learning, knowledge and insight, and capable of taking a place in the king's palace" (1:4). They are people who will already have received some education to prepare them for political life; they are thus well-versed in that practical Israelite learning such as appears in Proverbs. So that they can function in *his* court, Nebuchadnezzar determines to teach them also "the language and literature of the Chaldeans" (1:4)—the language, script, and contents of the cuneiform texts preserved among the Babylonian sages, which formed the basis of their work as court counselors.

These sages combined many of the functions of wise men, prophets, and priests in Israel. They were the guardians of the sacred traditional lore of Mesopotamia, which covered natural history, astronomy, mathematics, medicine, myth, and chronicle. This learning was applied to life by means of the study of the stars, of dreams, and of animal livers and other organs, and by means of rites of purification, sacrifice, incantation, exorcism, and other forms of divination and magic.

Their work presupposed that supernatural forces sometimes reveal what is to happen in the future, or unveil the significance of events which have already happened, either of their own accord or in response to human questioning. They were thought to do this through the arrangement of natural phenomena such as the stars or through the form or behavior of particular creatures. In light of such revelations, afflictions could be removed or threatened events avoided by means of the appropriate rites. By applying their learning in such ways to questions affecting king and nation, the sages acted as advisers and protectors whom the king would frequently consult (as Dan 2, 4, 5 presuppose). They comprised the king's backup agencies and task forces, able to access vast information resources to enable them to interpret data which might have implications for the future of the state.

A number of names are used for the various groups of sages, such as diviners, chanters, charmers, Chaldeans, and exorcists (see 1:20; 2:2, 27). The terms seem to be used randomly and interchangeably. The very variety of the names of the groups underlines both the anxiety built into the situation when they were summoned and the mockery with which the Israelites are invited to view the Babylonians' toilsome attempts to control their destiny (cf. Isa 47:12, 13).[1]

The Old Testament is not opposed to divination and its associated rites as such; it rather claims that Yahweh has more distinctive and more direct ways of communicating with Israel. Thus while Nebuchadnezzar wishes the young Judeans to profit from Chaldean learning, their God has other ideas. They receive "knowledge and discernment in all kinds of literature and learning" such as make them ten times superior to all the sages in Nebuchadnezzar's realm (1:17–20): a bold claim, whether in a Babylonian, a Persian, or a Greek context. As God's gift, then, the four men's insight has ceased to be merely rational/experiential court wisdom of the kind that can be learned, and has become supernaturally revealed knowledge such as they will be showing in succeeding chapters.

Not for nothing will Daniel come to be called a prophet, in the Dead Sea Scrolls and in the New Testament. The Book of Daniel itself does not use the word of him, though this affirmation is virtually made by Nebuchadnezzar himself later when he declares that "the spirit of holy deity" is in Daniel (4:8). While the Bible sometimes envisages God's spirit working in the human spirit through the ordinary analytical functioning of the human mind, it more characteristically associates the activity of God's spirit with the receiving of extraordinary insights such as one might associate with intuition, creative imagination, or second sight. A person who receives out-of-the-ordinary insights or revelations does so by the work of the spirit of God, as Joseph illustrates (Gen 41:38). Remarkable words are taken to have been breathed out by God's own breath.

Still later, in Belshazzar's day, the queen mother also recalls how the divine spirit dwelt in Daniel, though she sets alongside this theological description an anthropological one, of Daniel as a man with a remarkable spirit. She also speaks of how he had been found by Nebuchadnezzar to be a person of "insight" or divinely-given illumination, of "ability" which turned an intellectual skill into a practical skill, of "wisdom" in the sense of supernatural intuition, and of "knowledge" in the sense of God-given perceptiveness, all of which enabled him to interpret dreams, enigmas like the writing on the wall, and other opaque forms of divine revelation (5:11, 12), in the way that the sages were supposed to.

By allowing the four men to be exposed to alien wisdom but then portraying their God-given insight as superior, the Book of Daniel makes the same point as Isaiah 47 with its overt attack on Babylonian divination. Indeed, it perhaps makes it more strongly. It affirms that there is insight about life, history, and politics (the affairs the young men are concerned with) that only God endows. Members of the Israelite royal family have been taken into the service of the Babylonian king but they have found themselves in a position of leadership at his court, not through military or political achievement but through God-given wisdom.[2]

Insight as God's own attribute

It is the story of Nebuchadnezzar's dream statue that gives us our first concrete portrait of Babylonian and Israelite insight at work. In the Bible, as elsewhere in the ancient world, dreams are featured both as ordinary human experiences and as a means God uses to communicate with people. In neither are they the most common source of such data, but they were familiar enough to people. When God speaks in dreams, it may be a straightforward verbal message or it may be one expressed in symbols which require interpretation. Nebuchadnezzar's sages possessed extensive dream books listing dream motifs and their meanings. His summoning of the sages implies that his dream is assumed to be of state significance—it is not just an ordinary private dream, but an omen significant for the destiny of his empire. His anxiety reflects the insecurity which attaches to that empire.

The sages can hardly believe their ears, however, when they discover that Nebuchadnezzar expects them to tell him not only the meaning of his dream but its actual content. Their profession involves applying the insights of tradition and experience to data which the king gives them. But their confession of helplessness once the king requires them to move beyond textbook answers to set questions undermines the validity of the answers they provide within those parameters and raises the question whether their whole profession is a sham. If they can divine the contents of Nebuchadnezzar's dream, their understanding of its meaning compels respect. If not, the latter is no more than ordinary human opinion.

They do not claim to be privy to the secrets of the gods (2:11). But the wistful, sad admission by which they thus seek to excuse themselves exposes them and judges them (cf. the contempt expressed in Isa 44:25; also Jer 23:15–32). Jewish exiles might be tempted to fear that Israelite wisdom looked foolish in comparison with the resources of the sages. Actually the Babylonians have only earthly techniques which are no heavenly use (in the absence of data) and heavenly beings who are no earthly use. The this-worldly insight of the sages cannot compete with the supernatural insight of Daniel. The motif of the sages' helplessness recurs in the Belshazzar story (5:8), driving home this key point that alien wisdom is helpless when God intervenes to speak and act.

Indeed, the story of Nebuchadnezzar's dream shows that the so-called sages also lack the diplomatic skill to handle the king with adroitness, and even fail to get their way when they want time (to devise a solution to the king's conundrum); Daniel gets time (to seek a revelation from God). His courageous undertaking to provide an answer recalls his instinctive boldness regarding the trial (1:12), while his decisiveness and calm confidence contrasts with the sages' incredulous impotence.

So Daniel and his friends lay hold on the resources there are in their God, and the mystery is revealed to Daniel (2:19). His responsive praise ironically takes up the sages' confession that their gods' dwelling is not among mere humanity (2:11), and denies that this makes God inaccessible. God is one who possesses knowledge and insight. In particular, God understands history—the area the dream might be expected to concern. As the One who controls history, God has insight into history; as the One who has insight into history, God can reveal its significance; as the One who actually can reveal the significance of history, God is proved to be the One who controls history (2:20–23).

Like Isaiah 40–55, Daniel denies that insight into history comes from the stars that the Babylonian sages studied, as if they shaped history. History is God's secret, and cannot be predicted or divined by means of techniques such as those of the sages—as they have now acknowledged. It can only be revealed. Even Daniel does not reveal it merely because he is a more skilful sage, but because he is granted access to supernatural sources of information (2:30). Again Daniel resembles Joseph (Gen 41:16), whose portrait at many points anticipates Daniel's. The reason Babylonian wisdom can be scorned is that something that works is now available. Contrary to the despairing assumption of the sages, who believed that there were gods in heaven but did not think they revealed themselves, the Book of Daniel makes the key assertion that the God of heaven reveals secrets.

The insight expressed in quasi-prophecy

What is it that God reveals? Daniel's visions offer a series of previews of the history to unfold after Daniel's day. The most detailed is the prophecy in Daniel 11 which outlines the rise, activities, achievements, and fall of a series of kings. They are unnamed, but can be identified on the basis of the events the visions refer to (see chapter 1 above and chapter 8 below). Such prophecies have no parallels elsewhere in the Bible, but there are a number of parallels outside it from Mesopotamia, Egypt, and Greece, from the late second millennium to the Hellenistic period and after. One Assyrian example reads

. . . a ruler will arise, he will rule for thirteen years.
There will be an attack of Elam against Akkad, and
the booty of Akkad will be carried off.
The temples of the great gods will be destroyed, the
    defeat of Akkad will
be decreed [by the gods].
There will be confusion, disturbance, and unhappy
    events in the land, and
the reign will diminish [in power];
another man, whose name is not mentioned [as a
    successor] will arise, and
will seize the throne as king and will put to death his
    officials . . .[3]

Such "prophecies," offering descriptions in predictive form of the reigns of various unnamed kings, seem to be quasi-predictions, not actual predictions. For the most part they relate events from before the speaker's day as if they were future events. Only near the end do they express actual expectations or hopes of the prophet's day.

It would, of course, be possible for God to reveal to Daniel ahead of time the events of the next four centuries, and this is what Jewish and Christian scholars have generally assumed he did. But in light of the parallels just referred to, it seems that the people to whom the visions in Daniel were related would not take them as actual predictions. They would know that such prophecies had the form of quasi-predictions, not actual predictions, until they would come to the promises of deliverance toward the end. They would not assume that they were directly given by Daniel, but rather that they came from some unnamed seer of their own day (though they might reckon that Daniel himself was speaking through this seer: the phrase "I, Daniel" which recurs in Daniel 7 suggests this, as it is characteristically a phrase used by a person who cannot be seen or who speaks through someone else such as a prophet or a messenger).

They might also have reflected that the God of the Bible is not inclined to reveal the details of the future in the way that would be required if these were actual predictions rather than quasi-predictions. God expects people to live and walk by faith (see Matt 24:36; Acts 1:7). Further, God is characteristically one who speaks to people in their own situation, not to other people about it centuries beforehand in a way that is not directly relevant then. Ezekiel's contemporaries dismissed at least one of his visions on the grounds that it related to distant days. Ezekiel himself knew that God does not speak about distant days; God's promises and warnings relate to that future which is coming upon a prophet's hearers (see Ezek 12:27, 28).

So even if we did not have these ancient Middle-Eastern texts which reveal to us how the Jews would have understood detailed "prophecies" of this kind, we would have suspected that they were more likely quasi-prophecies than actual ones. The apparent exceptions in Daniel to the rule that God declines to speak to people in detail about the distant future merely prove the rule, because the visions actually date from the 160s and concern for the most part events which are present and imminent, not distant, for seer and audience.

The other visions in Daniel 7–12 are also quasi-prophecies, though not all of precisely the same kind. Daniel 7 and 8, for instance, incorporate motifs from myth, symbol, and allegory as well as scriptural allusion (see chapter 7 below). Symbols suggest features of the entity being described (Antiochus = a horn = something aggressive and strong), but they also bring with them resonances from sacred tradition.

The prophecies concerning postexilic history in Daniel are thus revelations from God in a similar sense as the Old Testament histories are. Both visionaries and historians acquired their knowledge about historical events in the same way, from personal experience or from historical sources; but both offer a God-given understanding of these events. Historians then tell of these events in the past tense, seers speak of them as if they are still future.

The revelations in Daniel 10–12 and elsewhere are substantially shaped by the Scriptures themselves: it was these Scriptures which mediated the author's God-given understanding to him. Among key passages which influence the revelation are Ezekiel 1–3, 9, 10 (in the introductory vision in Dan 10); Isaiah 8:7, 8, 10; Ezekiel 7:19–27; and Habakkuk 2:3 (in the historical presentation in Dan 11); and Isaiah 26:19; 52:13–53:12; and 66:24 (in the portrait of the End in Dan 12). It is the Scriptures which are the seer's source of insight. They enable him to make sense of past, present, and future for his people. The past they have been through (the rule of foreign empires over Judea, the comings and goings of the Hellenistic period, the sufferings of the Antiochene period) seems impossible to understand, but Scripture helps the seer to make sense of them. The Seleucid oppression is like that of the Assyrians: as the latter fell, so will the former. The temple desecration is like that during the Exile: as that was reversed, so will this one be. The affliction brought upon people by Antiochus is like that of Yahweh's servant in Isaiah: in this case, too, it will give way to triumph.

The fact that the quasi-predictions can make sense of the past by relating it in the light of Scripture implies grounds for trusting the actual prophecy's interpretation of what the future will hold (11:40–12:4). When the seer speaks about the past, he does so on the basis of having historical data and having the scriptural text as a means of interpreting it. When he speaks about the future, he has only scriptural text (because God does expect people to walk by faith) and he is providing an imaginary scenario, a possible embodiment of the biblical text, which is not designed to be pressed to yield historical data. The fact that Antiochus does not die as 11:40–45 describes does not prove it is a failed prophecy, or a prophecy about someone other than Antiochus which is yet to be fulfilled. Its object is to provide not historical data but scriptural insight on the *meaning* of events to come.

Visions regularly use familiar forms, and the fact that this one uses the form of the quasi-prediction need not suggest any doubt regarding whether it was a genuine vision. God reaches people through means that speak to them, and the form of quasi-predictions was one which could reach the seer and speak to his people. It provided them with a very vivid way of affirming that puzzling events which have taken place really are within the control and purview of God.

The seer thus seeks to provide insight on contemporary Jewish experience by looking at it in the light of various scriptural texts. It is this insight which is mediated to the body of faithful Jews by "the discerning" (or "teachers," as the term could alternatively be taken) (11:33), leaders who possess that wisdom which consists in awed submission to God, that understanding which has reflected deeply on God's ways in history, and that insight which perceives how God's cause will ultimately triumph.[4] They use this to "enlighten the multitude," an activity which apparently denotes not teaching in general or exhortation to faithfulness but the interpretation of the prophetic Scriptures for the persecuted community.

The picture of a heavenly being reading off from a book the contents of coming centuries might seem to imply a strongly deterministic view of history. The march of the kingdoms is the march of toy soldiers programed by God.[5] If this were so, one might have reckoned that God could have programed it better! But the awareness that these are quasi-prophecies gives us a helpful new perspective on this aspect of Daniel's attitude toward history. Only retrospectively do the visions affirm God's "control." Events are described as inevitable (11:14, 27) when they *are* inevitable—when they have already happened. We have noted that when the vision turns to describing the actual future, it offers an imaginative scenario rather than a literal forecast, and this itself reflects the fact that events are not imposed on humanity but emerge from their will. God will not be frustrated regarding the destiny of history, but events themselves unfold in the ordinary way that history does. It is with hindsight that one declares that everything that has taken place—even the hard things the people have gone through—is within the hand of God. To say that history was prewritten is to deny that it is out of control.

5   DANIEL'S GOD AND DANIEL'S PRAYER

The Book of Daniel contains three key references to Daniel's prayer—one in the context of his needing God to reveal Nebuchadnezzar's dream to him (Dan 2), one as the activity which involves his disobeying Darius (Dan 6), one as his plea for God to restore Israel from their exile (Dan 9). They are prayers which involve petition, intercession, confession, and thanksgiving. The three accounts thus disclose central features of the nature of prayer. They also draw attention to central aspects of the character of the God to whom we pray.

Petition and intercession

Nebuchadnezzar insists that the sages tell him about the dream whose contents he will not or cannot specify, and Daniel makes an audacious, precipitate declaration that he will indeed do so. *Then* he goes home to get his friends to pray about it (2:16–18)! Literally he wants them "to ask for compassion" from God: that is the nature of prayer. The

Hebrew and Aramaic words for "compassion" (English translations often use the word "mercy") are related to words for the womb. They suggest the strong feelings of love and concern appropriate to brothers and sisters from the same womb or to a mother in relation to the children of her womb. So the God to whom we pray is one who has the caring instincts of a brother or sister or mother for us.

On the second occasion when Daniel petitions his God, the story describes him as "seeking grace" (6:11). "Grace" is another term from personal relationships, in the family or elsewhere. It suggests the caring favor that one person may show to another even though they have no legal obligation to them. Prayer involves casting oneself on the divine favor when we have no claim on God, and pleading with the God of grace.

Alongside these words in the prayer in Daniel 9:4 comes the word "commitment" (English translations have expressions such as "steadfast love"). In secular usage this word is more at home in life outside the family, in connection with relationships in the community and in political life. It is a word which denotes an attitude of kindness or generosity or mercy which expresses itself in acts of that kind and which thus initiates or presupposes a relationship of mutual loyalty and faithfulness between people. Applied to God, it appears most commonly in the context of prayer, in an appeal to the commitment inherent in the nature of God.

"Faithfulness" (or "reliability" or "constancy") (9:13) commonly accompanies "commitment" in the Old Testament, in references to God and to human conduct. Together "commitment" and "faithfulness" suggest a steadfastness which can be relied on; in contradistinction from each other, they indicate on the one hand active kindness which gives what is good, and on the other protective faithfulness which guards from harm. In Daniel 9:13 the history of Israel is the story of

God's faithfulness to Israel: God's promises have been reliable, God's protection has been constant.

The history of Israel can also be described as the story of God's "right deeds" (9:16); these are themselves acts of faithfulness, mercy, commitment and deliverance. The paradigm act of this kind is the Exodus (9:15), the event which established Yahweh's reputation for doing the right thing. So prayer is an appeal to God to do the right thing.

That second occasion when Daniel petitions his God takes him into the lion pit, because people are forbidden to petition anyone but the king. His prayer is unusual even apart from its bravery (see 6:11, 12). The regular hours for prayer were the times of the morning and evening offering, especially the latter (cf. 9:21). Daniel, however, is accustomed to praying three times a day; we have no other reference in the Bible to anyone doing that (assuming that Psalm 55:17 is not describing someone's regular practice of prayer, any more than is the case with the "seven times" of Psalm 119:164).

The regular posture for prayer was standing (e.g., Mark 11:25). Daniel, however, kneels to pray, implying prostrating himself as Muslims do; normally someone would only do that as an indication of marked self-lowering in circumstances of particular solemnity or need. His praying "before his God" also suggests a meekness in the presence of authority: it is the term used in connection with addressing the king (e.g., 2:9, 10, 11), though at the same time it thus indicates the actuality of standing in a real person's presence. Having an attic which could be used for a private meeting, for guests, or for prayer, would also be unusual; ordinary people would have a makeshift shelter on the roof for these purposes.

Facing the land, the city, and the temple during prayer is emphasized throughout Solomon's prayer in 1 Kings 8 but is referred to rarely elsewhere outside Daniel. It may be that "turning to God" (9:3), too, indicates facing Jerusalem, but that expression also implies that Daniel's prayer is a deliberate, purposeful act. The phrase is literally "to set the face"; it denotes determination when confronted by a crisis or a challenge. The deliberateness involved in such prayer is also suggested by Daniel's describing it as "laying down" supplications, or causing them to fall, before Yahweh (9:20)—another expression which may hint at prostration of the self before God.

So Daniel is set forward as an amazing man of prayer, but also as an example of prayer to which, in some respects at least, others might aspire. They too belong to another city (despite Jeremiah 29) and need outward ways of demonstrating to themselves as much as to others the fact that they live as strangers among the Chaldeans, whether they actually feel secure or insecure there.[1]

Daniel's account of his prayer of confession illustrates further how prayer can be a matter of actions as well as words. The actions add to the sense of seriousness and earnestness expressed by the words. Fasting, sackcloth, and ashes (9:3) are recognized indications of grief and self-abasement in the context of calamity or loss experienced or threatened, or of wrongdoing committed. Fasting involved abstaining from (regular) food during the day (not usually for the whole twenty-four hours). Sackcloth was dark, rough, cheap material worn in contrast to the more presentable smart clothing in which someone would normally want to appear in public. The reference to ashes denotes the practice of putting ashes (or dust or soil) on the head or head and body, or of lying or sitting in a pile of ashes.

The background of such practices presumably lies in the way shock, loss, and grief naturally express themselves in a loss of interest in food and appearances, and in an inner gloominess which expresses itself outwardly in "the blues." The practices themselves give formal, stylized, ritual expression to feelings people have or purport to have.

Fasting also features in the context of a special meeting with God, or the seeking of a meeting with God or a revelation from God (cf. 10:2, 3). Here there is no suggestion of loss or grief; fasting indicates an abandoning of normal human preoccupations for the sake of concentration on seeking God or being with God. So Daniel's fasting may be seen as both an expression of grief, to accompany his plea for divine action, and as an indication of seriousness in seeking God, to accompany his plea for divine revelation.

At the same time it is striking that Daniel's period of self-denial is coterminous with the period of conflict among the supernatural powers (10:2, 13). This hints that prayer can play a role in opening up the possibility of God's purpose being fulfilled when human purposes conflict with that. Daniel's seeking God on Israel's behalf "opened an aperture for God to act in concert with human freedom. It inaugurated war in heaven. It opened a way through the impenetrable spirituality of a foreign hegemony in order to declare a new and real divine possibility."[2]

The Old Testament assumes that prayers meet with responses, and Daniel's prayer in chapter 9 does receive one. The point expressed in loving hyperbole in Isaiah 65:24 (cf. 65:1) here becomes prosaic narrative reality: God is so eager to respond to prayer (and the divine sovereignty in human affairs is so real) that the response comes before the prayer is actually over (9:20, 21). The prayer offered the response to God's prophetic word which made the fulfillment of that word possible. The promise of fulfillment issues when Daniel turns to God, yet it issues before he actually prays his lament, so that the story affirms not only the importance of prayer and the place it has in the outworking of God's purpose (it is in response to prayer that God acts) but also the importance of God's sovereignty (prayer is a means of God's own good will being put into effect). One person's prayer brings about the restoration of the people of God; but it is a matter of releasing that restoration which God has already purposed.

Thanksgiving

The thanksgiving Daniel offers when his first prayer is answered (2:20-23) parallels those of the Psalms and uses their phrases and motifs. But its specific content recalls less the Psalms than Job (e.g., 1:21; 12:22; 32:8; 38:19)—another book which portrays the feelings and prayers of an individual rather than being a liturgical composition like the Psalms themselves.

The thanksgiving begins, however, with a very liturgical blessing of God, like those at the end of the books of the Psalter (e.g., Ps 72:18, 19). To bless someone is to express in solemn words one's appreciation, gratitude, honor, recognition, or love; it suggests an acknowledgment of communion with the one who is named in the blessing, in the light of what they have come to mean to you.[3] Praise applies this way of speaking to God.

The object of Daniel's blessing is the "God of heaven" (2:19). Such titles for deities are common throughout Old Testament times among peoples such as the Canaanites, the Babylonians, the Persians, and the Greeks. In using them, Israelites indicate that their God is not merely an Israelite peculiarity but the sovereign Lord, the one whom other peoples "ignorantly worship" (see Acts 17:23, 24) insofar as they truly worship God at all. Israelites may also be glad to use such expressions for God because they thus avoid the actual name "Yahweh." In some circles after the Exile people came to avoid the name because they wanted to be sure they did not misuse it (cf. Exod 20:7); the name hardly appears in Daniel outside chapter 9. So here "the God of heaven" may be a reverential substitute for God's actual name (cf. Matthew's use of the phrase "the kingdom of heaven" for "the kingdom of God").

The phrase "the name of God" (2:20) is another expression which enables people to avoid actually saying "Yahweh." It presupposes the way that someone's name often revealed something of their character or personal significance. As with human beings, then, God's name stood for God's person. One reason for using the title "the God of my fathers" (2:23) may also be the desire to avoid the actual name of God. In its own right, though, this description of God suggests that one is committed to Israel's traditional faith, the faith handed down by their forebears, and that one believes that the God who first became involved with Israel long ago is faithful to the children now, as to the forebears then. The title "God Most High" is yet another expression which likely came into increasing usage partly because it provided an alternative to the name "Yahweh."

In the accustomed fashion of a blessing, after the actual declaration of it there follows a brief statement of the reason for it: "wisdom and might are his." The twofold confession is expanded in verses 21, 22. Then the blessing returns to explicit thanksgiving, relating it to the same two divine characteristics, which have become not merely God's possession but God's gift to Daniel personally. The personal nature of the praise is developed in the rest of verse 23 as it focuses more on the particular event which prompted this thanksgiving.

To put it another way, the end of Daniel's praise is more explicitly like thanksgiving, the confession of what God has done for me/us in response to my/our urgent plea. In form, the beginning part could be the kind of praise that comes in a hymn where the concern is with acknowledging God's characteristic attributes and actions. But specific experiences of God's acting on their behalf feeds and strengthens their affirmations regarding those characteristic attributes and actions. God has answered Daniel's prayer, and this is the praise such an experience generates.

A dramatic effect is achieved by the way Daniel's thanksgiving is recorded at this point in Daniel 2. His confession of God's power and wisdom comes before his indicating the content of what God has actually revealed to him. Daniel is to speak of the destiny of Nebuchadnezzar's empire, a revelation which will evidence that power and wisdom of the God of heaven. Most of the time the people of God have to live without revelations of this kind, yet they are still called to confess, with Daniel, that power and wisdom on the basis of a revelation which they believe will come but which they have not yet seen. Even if we do not see much evidence of the might and wisdom of God in international affairs, we are called to believe in that wisdom and power yet to be revealed, and to thank God for it even before we see it.

A related point emerges from the description of Daniel as being "in prayer and thanksgiving" in Daniel 6. The combination of terms suggests two mutually dependent major aspects of praying (cf. Phil 4:6). Daniel evidently interweaves his pleas (for Israel, for himself, for the Babylonian state) with testimony to his conviction that God hears and answers—the central confession of the Psalms, which is indicated by the term "thanksgiving." Daniel is confident that the living God knows his situation and peril and has already determined how to preserve him through it; he is confident of that not least because of the personal experience he already has of God's responding to him in times of need, which his thanksgiving recalls.

Confession

The longer prayer in Daniel 9 arises out of the reading of Scripture, and illustrates the interplay there can be between the words of Scripture and the words of prayer, as Scripture stimulates prayer and prayer forms the appropriate response to Scripture. It is a confession like those in Ezra 9 and in Nehemiah 1, 9. Practically every phrase can be paralleled in other such instances of prayers of confession. It instinctively but also consciously follows a hallowed and traditional way of praying, probably as known both from the study and the worship of the synagogue. The reality of the individual's experience of life and of God keeps the prayer of the ongoing community alive and real; the tradition of the community's prayer over the centuries gives the individual's prayer its means of expression and its context in the prayer of the whole community of faith.

In his way of speaking, Daniel alternates between "we/our" and "I/my," and between "you" and "he" in referring to God. It is a prayer of confession prayed on behalf of the whole people, so that "we/our" is appropriate. But Daniel is in the position of such intercessors as Moses and Jeremiah, and thus his "I/my" is also natural.

His confession addresses God as "Lord," as "Yahweh," as "my God," and as "our God." Only in this prayer does Daniel use God's personal name "Yahweh," which constitutes an appeal in prayer to the special relationship between Yahweh and the people who alone knew that name. But the prayer also uses the title "Lord" at a number of points where Israelite prayer would traditionally have used "Yahweh." Given that this also reflects the developing inclination in Judaism to avoid uttering the actual name of God, the occurrences of the title "Lord" are suggestive of reverence in prayer before the majesty of God.

Appeal to a special relationship with God also underlies the references to "our God" and "my God." Daniel uses "my God" in referring to his own prayer, "our God" when he refers to those for whom he prays. He appeals to "my God" (the one who grants special revelations to him) to act as "our

God" (see especially 9:18-20 for the personal nature of Daniel's appeal on behalf of the people as a whole).

The prayer begins with praise of "the great and awesome God who keeps his covenantal commitment with people who love him and keep his commands" (9:4). There is a courageous realism about beginning a prayer of confession with a recognition of the majesty of God, a threat to those who fail to yield to it; it is such failure that Daniel will have to go on to acknowledge. The fact that God is also one who keeps covenantal commitment does not take the edge off this; it is a recognition that any failure with regard to the covenant relationship is Israel's, not God's. On the other hand, the fact that Israel's relationship with God began from God's unearned commitment to Israel might open up the possibility that it could be reestablished on the same basis.

Recognition that right is on Yahweh's side is a key element in a prayer such as this. It presupposes an acknowledgment of facts as they are. Our description of the recognition of sin as "confession" is suggestive, because we also speak of "confession" of faith: the essence of confession is the (public) acknowledgment of facts, to the glory of God. Confession of sin is thus a strange form of praise, an act of praise at the justice of the judgment of God.[4]

The central part of the prayer of confession is the actual acknowledgment of wrongdoing (9:5-14). It takes the form of a statement in general terms of what the people have done and failed to do, a statement of God's acts in response, and a contrasting of the consequent moral positions of God and people ("right belongs to you, Lord, while a look of shame attaches to us," 9:7). Yahweh had given the people of Israel as a whole authoritative commands and directives through Moses and through the prophets; these were delivered to kings, leaders of tribes and clans, and rulers of the local community. But they have not loved God or kept God's commands (the second phrase reminds us that the verb "love" denotes as much a moral as an emotional commitment).

Admittedly, an element of disobedience on their part was inevitable and not fatal to their relationship with Yahweh. If they had "turned" from wrongdoing (the standard Hebrew expression for repentance) they could "seek mercy from Yahweh"—or, more literally, persuade Yahweh to take a warm and favorable attitude toward them—so that the relationship would continue (9:13).

They have not even done that. Indeed, they (leaders and people, present generation and past generations who continue to influence the present) have willfully fallen short of God's expectations, avoided walking in the way God prescribed, ignored the claims God had on them, rebelled against God's authority, trespassed on God's rights, overstepped God's instruction, turned their backs on God's commands, closed their ears to God's warnings. As a result Yahweh has with personal deliberateness and careful consideration, but also with burning fury, ensured that the curse of which they were warned has overwhelmed them. Thus their present experience is trouble, desolation, mourning, dishonor, and banishment.

The acknowledgment of being in the wrong opens the way to a plea for mercy, a prayer for God to turn back to the people in forgiveness and restoration (9:15-19: most movingly in the closing clauses, 9:19). Its most fundamental petition is that God may "listen" (repeated in verses 17-19). That is the standard first plea in a lament, for the nature of such prayer is that it arises out of a context where God seems to have been ignoring Israel's plight and her prayer. The other standard feature of the prayer in a lament is the appeal to God to act—here to turn away the burning divine fury from the city, to let God's face shine on the sanctuary instead, to look, to pardon, and to act without delay.

The plea is dominated by clauses and phrases that indicate the reasons why that should happen. It bases itself on the pattern of God's activity in the past, always doing the "right" thing. To do the "right" thing is to do the "just" thing; but God's justice is not one concerned above all to see wickedness punished. To abandon anger at Israel's wrongdoing (9:16) would now be in keeping with Yahweh's just deeds, not in conflict with them. Yahweh's justice indicates a concern for what is right which rejoices in being merciful to the weak; and people who suffer as a result of sin are still seen as people who suffer and need to be restored.

Secondly, the plea bases itself on God's compassion. Although "compassion" is a feelings word, it denotes feelings which issue in action, the action here being the willingness to "pardon" (9:19—not the usual word for "forgive," which can be used of human forgiveness, but a word only used of God, and suggesting pardon by a superior).

> The Israel which acknowledges its God's justice even when disaster comes to it can ask for his mercy. Only those who know that they are struck down as guilty before God, only they can appeal to God's mercy.[5]

Thirdly, the plea bases itself on the fact that city and people bear God's name—that is, they belong to Yahweh. With Yahweh's own encouragement, Israel had depicted Jerusalem as the very center of the world. Its desolation put a question mark by such theological assertions. But these assertions involved God's own name. God has to restore Jerusalem. As W. S. Towner comments:

> To the degree that he has committed himself to preserving the safety of those things which are named by his name . . . the God of Israel has limited and compromised his own freedom to act in the future.[6]

Prayers of confession such as that in Daniel 9 belong to a covenantal way of thinking, one which understands the relationship between God and human beings by analogy with those human relationships which are based on a formal agreement entered into in solemn and binding fashion. It is this which may explain a difference from earlier Old Testament prayers for restoration. While the prayer incorporates some description of the afflicted state of the people for whom Daniel prays, material corresponding to the lament in a psalm of lament—complaint and protest with their characteristic "why?"—have disappeared in the light of the covenantal thinking which pervades a prayer such as this. The reason for suffering is not God's neglect but God's justice.[7]

The prayer is an acknowledgment of the covenantal God, of the breaking of the covenant through Israel's failure to keep covenant commitment, and of the appropriateness of God's treatment of Israel in the framework of the covenant. Its appeal for mercy is based on the graciousness which lay behind God's own covenant commitment. It is based implicitly on the possibility of forgiveness and restoration announced in the covenant for people who, when punished and exiled, repent of their covenant failure (see Leviticus 26; Deuteronomy 30).

If this is indeed how people prayed in those days, we can see how they came through the storms and stresses of that terrible time.[8]

6   THE POWERS OF HEAVEN

Figures whom we commonly refer to as "angels" feature more frequently in Daniel than in any other book in the Bible (though they are still less prominent in Daniel than in a near-contemporary Jewish work such as 1 Enoch). Further, even Daniel says little or nothing about the nature or origin of these heavenly beings, about how many of them there are or how they are ordered, or about distinctions between good and evil beings among them. What Daniel does say indicates that consideration of them requires more than jest or sentimentalism. They are not dainty figures in dresses but executives, messengers, and warriors whose very names (Michael, "Who is like God"; Gabriel, "Mighty man of God") sometimes draw attention to the uniqueness and might of God which they mediate.

God's representatives and aides acting on earth

To us, an angel is a figure who is clearly supernatural but also clearly distinguishable from God. The Greek word from which "angel" comes, however, means a messenger; it does not distinguish whether human or supernatural. The Hebrew and Aramaic term is the one which lies behind the name of the prophet Malachi, "my messenger": it, too, applies to a human as easily as to a heavenly being. It denotes not the being of someone but that person's role. They are representatives, who speak or act on God's behalf, mediating in the world the word and the will of God. The term "holy ones" can also be used to denote both heavenly and earthly figures (see Daniel 9).

When the term "messenger" does denote a heavenly being, it suggests not that this being is clearly distinct from God, but rather that it mediates the real presence of God. Thus in Genesis "the angel of Yahweh" and "Yahweh" can be hard to distinguish.

The relative prominence of these supernatural figures in Daniel does not imply that God is now felt as remote and inaccessible, any more than is the case when the Gospels and Acts stress the involvement of such beings in the story of Jesus and of the beginnings of the church. It provides a way of envisaging the means by which God governs the world. In a polytheistic faith different roles can be attributed to different gods, but Israel was aware that there was such a gulf between Yahweh and other supernatural beings that the same word hardly applied equally to both.

Talk in terms of the aides of God thus helps give expression to two truths about God. It portrays God as really involved in the world, speaking and acting; but it safeguards God's exaltedness and transcendent authority by visualizing God's speaking and acting as embodied in subordinate representatives, like those of the imperial authority.

If one says that God is (for instance) in the furnace rescuing the three young men (3:28) or in the lion pit with Daniel shutting the lions' mouths (6:22), one might seem to raise questions about how God could be also seated on the throne controlling the destiny of the whole universe. Israel had to affirm that Yahweh sat on the throne of heaven. It also had to affirm that Yahweh really spoke and acted on earth. Understanding Yahweh as speaking and acting via a representative or aide who brought the words of God and the power of God helped to safeguard both of these truths about God just referred to.

In the story of the red-hot blazing furnace, Nebuchadnezzar has already referred to the fourth figure in the furnace as a "divine being" (literally a "son of the gods"). Isaiah 43:1–3 had promised God's own presence when Israel walks through the fire. When that divine being, God's aide, joins the three young men, this promise is fulfilled.

Nebuchadnezzar's dream about the tree (Dan 4) portrays the activity of God by means of a more concrete analogy from the court. Within his administration the king had watchmen who were the eyes and ears whereby he controlled and provided for his realm. God's management of the affairs of heaven and earth is pictured by analogy with that of the human king; members of the divine council act as the eyes (Zech 4:10; 2 Chron 16:9) by which God keeps watch over the affairs of the realm and sees that the divine will is put into effect throughout it. The watchmen belong to heaven, are themselves supernatural beings, and bring the word of God. They descend from heaven and speak in the hearing of the earthly king, and thus implement the will of God on earth. The true ministry of angels is that of witnesses to God's work and word, to the God who alone rules.[1]

Gabriel and the man in linen bringing God's revelation

Gabriel (8:16; 9:21) is the first named angel in the Bible, though only one of a number who appear in older parts of 1 Enoch. He brings God's message to Daniel concerning the

The Powers of Heaven

limits to affliction. His human appearance is stressed (as we have noted, his name "mighty man of God" draws attention to it). It is thus unlikely that he is described as flying in Daniel 9:21. The notion that angels have wings derives from later confusion between angels, who are human in appearance, and cherubim or seraphim.

It may be Gabriel who appears again in Daniel 10, where we get the fullest account of heavenly beings bringing God's revelation. A man in linen appears to Daniel. Linen is the garb of a priest, so it seems here that the servant of the heavenly temple also concerns himself with the affairs of its earthly equivalent. But his appearance is of such dazzling brightness and awesome splendor (paralleling the appearance of God in Ezekiel 1, from which it derives) that it inspires a holy terror and deathlike trance in Daniel and his companions—almost as if they have seen God and all but lose their lives as a consequence.[2]

Although his role is similar to that of Gabriel, he has also been linked with the manlike figure of Daniel 7 and with Michael; but there are no specific grounds for identifying him with one of these figures. As in Daniel 7, the scene in Daniel 10 has the allusiveness which often characterizes vision reports and which no doubt characterizes the visionary experience itself, and we must accept this allusiveness, which heightens the awesomeness of what is described. Nor is it clear whether it is the man in linen who continues to speak in 10:16-20 or whether other figures speak there, though 12:5, 6 makes explicit that two other "men" are also present at the scene.

The leaders of the nations

Daniel 7 and 8 contain some allusive references to the heavenly army which is in some sense identified with Israel, but the theme is treated most explicitly (though still not entirely clearly) in Daniel 10, 11.

The Old Testament assumes that the results of battles on earth reflect the involvement of heaven. Usually the picture is of heavenly forces aiding Israel and enabling them to win against otherwise overwhelming earthly forces. When Israel loses, the presupposition will be that Yahweh fights against them. A few passages suggest that there are heavenly forces that oppose Yahweh, so that earthly battles reflect battles in heaven; whichever side wins in heaven, the equivalent wins on earth.

Daniel 10:13 and 10:20–11:1 describe a struggle between heavenly beings, though the nature of the struggle is again described allusively. Among those involved are the "leaders" or "kings" of Persia, Greece, and Israel; the passage uses ordinary Hebrew words for "leaders" and "kings" (as in 11:5) to refer in each case to a celestial being. Perhaps that hints at the idea that all entities that embody power have something human, earthly, structural, political, and visible about them, and also something heavenly, invisible, suprahuman, immaterial, and spiritual. They have an inner and an outer aspect, an outer form and an inner driving spirit. Israel's leader is Michael (an ordinary Hebrew name); he is also described as "one of the supreme leaders."

The conflict in heaven might be a verbal, legal one (cf. Zech 3) or might be a "physical" one. The speaker himself is acting as God's messenger to Daniel, but he is also involved in the conflict in heaven—hence his return to resume the fight to ensure that Persia continues to be restrained from adversely affecting God's purpose. But he warns that in due course the Greek leader will seek to implement his own purpose—that will be the heavenly equivalent to the Greeks attempting to implement their will, which also threatens God's purpose.

It is not that Persians or Greeks are consciously against God or against Israel; Israel just happens to be in their way. The messenger and Michael are on the same side because of the messenger's general concern with the fulfillment of God's purpose and because of Michael's particular involvement with Israel. This is thus not the first occasion when they have made common purpose (11:1).

Daniel does not think about history in a dualistic way. He is quite clear that God is sovereign in heaven and on earth. No other power rivals God. The divine purpose can be opposed and delayed, but not frustrated. Nor does Daniel imply that the real decisions about history are made in heaven, so that human acts make no difference to what happens. The revelation about Hellenistic history which follows makes clear that human beings are responsible for history. Armies have to fight as if the battle on the earthly plane alone counts. On the other hand, monistic thinking about history, which is more usual in our world, is an oversimplification. History is not merely the outworking of human decisions. Not only do free human decisions contribute to the achievement of God's purpose. The purposes of kings and nations are more than merely the decisions of particular human beings. Something in the realm of the spirit lies behind them.

So the idea of the leaders of the nations provides a way of thinking about history as people actually experience it. History involves conflicts between peoples, which seem to reflect more than merely human factors—for instance, it involves unexpected victories in which one is inclined to see the hand of God and unexpected defeats in which the promises of God seem not to be fulfilled. The power of the leader of Persia mirrors Persia's actual political power. The idea of the leaders of the nations is a way of expressing the fact that there is more to history and to reality than we can see: both individuals and states are more than merely themselves as historical realities.

The leaders must somehow be under God's ultimate control. They are not demonic opponents. But neither are they simply God's heavenly obedient servants. The job of the leader of Persia is to represent Persian interests in a world in conflict. "It has the right to contest for the best interests of the Persian empire narrowly defined"; the leaders are not "idealized personifications" of their nations, but "represent the actual spirituality and possibilities of actual entities."[3]

The notion of conflict between the nations' "leaders" also links with another experience we have with history. Often events work out *despite* the intentions of the nations rather than through them. What nations do, for good or ill, is not always what they were planning to do. It is as if some power other than themselves shapes their destiny. The Old Testament, of course, believes that Yahweh is this ultimate power. We will consider this theme further as we ponder the way Daniel looks at history.

7 PERSPECTIVES ON HISTORY

We have seen in chapter 1 that this short book encompasses an extraordinarily wide historical sweep. History is not merely its background and context but its subject. It is concerned with the meaning of history and with the relationship between God and history. In particular, it offers a series of portrayals and assessments of Middle-Eastern history beginning with the Exile.

*History in its richness and diversity, its
unity and weakness*

In Daniel 2, history to come is portrayed in a vision concerning a statue made of four metals, which together sum up the variety of valuable natural resources. Gold and silver suggest what is majestic and precious, bronze and iron suggest what is strong and hard. The elements of the statue stand for regimes which are to rule the Middle East, though the precise identity of these is not made specific. As we shall see, the identification of the four regimes in Daniel 7 is easier; they are a sequence of empires lasting from the sixth century B.C. to the second. But one cannot necessarily infer (as interpreters generally do) that the interpretation of Daniel 7 can be read back into Daniel 2.

I myself think it is more likely that Daniel 2 refers to a sequence of sixth-century kings. But it is important to grasp that Daniel 2 is more allusive than Daniel 7, and that no one can really be dogmatic about it. The point it is making does not depend on identifying the precise regimes to which it is referring.

The statue stands for *four* regimes, and four is commonly a symbolic number suggesting completeness; it might not refer to precisely four reigns. The statue embodies a many-faceted power, splendor, strength, and impressiveness— until we come to the feet, partly made of clay pottery. This alien element suggests weakness and transience, the antithesis of the power and strength indicated by the metals. It threatens the stability of the otherwise powerful edifice which towers above it.

The unity of the statue implies that the empire which the statue represents is one empire, ruled at the moment by Nebuchadnezzar but destined to pass to a sequence of future rulers. It was Nebuchadnezzar who brought to an end the rule of Judah by the descendants of David through whom God had promised to rule there; he was the first gentile ruler directly to control Israel's destiny. Beginning in his day the Jews are part of secular history. Yet this does not mean that history is working against God's purpose and will. The sequence of Middle-Eastern kings under which the Jews will henceforth live stands under God's sovereignty in the same real, though indirect, way as Judah's own kings had. God sets these kings' story in motion; God terminates it.[1]

There is a Persian scheme parallel to that suggested by the statue, which also pictures human epochs by means of metals.

It is possible that this scheme sees the mixed iron-and-clay age as the period of domination by demons.[2]

Daniel makes a striking contrast; his message continues on the human plane, there being no suggestion of a cosmic dualism of good and evil forces, even when it speaks in terms of heavenly powers as well as earthly powers (see chapter 6). The rule of gentile peoples over Jews is God-given, yet it is ultimately to be brought to an end and replaced by the implementing of God's own direct rule (2:44). Postexilic history belongs to God as it unfolds and as it comes to its end.

History as a concentration of disorder

Daniel's vision of history is expressed on the broadest canvas in the vision in Daniel 7. It begins with the four winds of the heavens stirring up the Great Sea, from which there emerge one by one onto the shore four strange and fearsome animals. In ordinary speech, the four winds could be just the ordinary winds that come from the four points of the compass, while the Great Sea is a standard expression for the Mediterranean. Daniel's vision invites us, then, to stand with him near the shore of the Mediterranean at a spot such as the promontory at Jaffa where the waters crash onto the Rock of Andromeda. Gales whirl from every direction and arouse the sea to a turbulent swell. But the motifs of fearsome animals combined with those of wind and sea suggest that this is no ordinary seaside scene: they recall mythic material from Babylon and Canaan already reflected in earlier parts of the Old Testament.

There is a famous Babylonian account of how the world came to be created, which tells of rebellious monsters born from the primeval ocean, and of the sea monster being destroyed by being burst by the winds. Similar motifs are featured in a parallel myth from Ugarit, a Canaanite city to the north of Israel. Here, too, the forces of chaos and disorder are embodied first in the Sea, then in the seven-headed dragon, Leviathan, which Baal, the hero of the story, defeats and kills.

In the Old Testament, motifs such as these appear in the Psalms, where the powers of evil asserting themselves in opposition to Israel and to God's concern for order are also represented by the sea or the sea monster, which God destroys (e.g., Pss 9; 29; 46; 93). They reappear in the prophets, who are more explicitly concerned with the way the forces of disorder are embodied in history when Israel experiences the collapse of order in the world (e.g., Isa 51:9, 10, in the context of the Exile). The author of Israel's own account of creation in Genesis 1 was apparently also aware of the Babylonian creation story, because at a number of points Genesis 1 seems to be combating the false Babylonian picture, which Jews in exile in Babylon might have been tempted to find impressive. And Genesis 1 begins with that supernatural power of God which is embodied in the wind hovering over the watery Deep—though the animals that the Word of God then calls forth are "good" rather than sinister.

Against this background, Daniel's talk of four winds, heaving sea, and huge animals must point to supernatural forces. The winds suggest the power of God effecting the will of God in history; the sea suggests the dense concentration of energy which threatens to disrupt and overwhelm order in history; the animals suggest the embodiment of that threatening energy in particular beings. *Four* winds and *four* animals indicate the world-encompassing totality of divine power and disorderly energy (cf. the fourfold stream of Gen 2:10).

The vision suggests both that the process of history is an unsavory, unnatural, dark, and unreassuring one, and that the entities which embody its disorder are nevertheless called forth by God. It is on this basis that Daniel's visions can join with the lament psalms in asking "How long will you make things work out this way?" There is a sense in which the whole of history is called forth by God, yet the bulk of it (as the sequence of animals suggests) proceeds in a way which reveals no pattern or meaning, and no salvation history.

The sequence begins with a creature that combines features of a lion, an eagle, and a man, a creature which stands for Babylon itself, the major power of Daniel's own day and the power that had actually terminated the independent national life of the people of Yahweh by abolishing its monarchy and ruling it from Babylon. It ends with a fearful and terrifying creature which is not likened to any other, as the first three creatures are; it may actually be an elephant. Evidently the fourth regime is again a powerful and violent one, particularly when headed by its final king, a man of arrogant spirit and persecuting tendency, symbolized by an extra, small horn which appears on the beast and grows to be very great. Who is this king?

In the next vision, which follows on in content from this one, the "small horn" (8:9; cf. 7:8) is clearly Antiochus Epiphanes. This suggests that the fourth regime in Daniel 7 is the Greek Empire and that here, if not in Daniel 2, the historical perspective of Daniel's vision indeed spans the period from the sixth century to the second (see further the discussion of Daniel 7 in chapter 8 below). The second and third animals might then stand for the Medo-Persian Empire and that of Alexander (the fourth denoting the Hellenistic empires which succeeded Alexander). More likely they stand for the Medes and the Persians considered as two separate empires (the fourth denoting the Greek empire as a whole).

Admittedly historians normally reckon these as one empire during this period, as other chapters of Daniel refer to Medo-Persian law as if the Medes and Persians are one rule. What is apparently happening here, however, is that Daniel's vision is utilizing a well-known "scheme" picturing history as divided into four ages, such as the one mentioned above in connection with the statue in Daniel 2. The author is not primarily concerned with literally precise history and is willing to "stretch" history in order to be able to use the scheme he wishes to adopt—as happens with the 490 years in Daniel 9, and with other figures elsewhere in Scripture (see e.g., the 480 years of 1 Kings 6:1 or the triple series of 14 generations in Matt 1).

History as an experience of wrath

As we have just noted, Daniel 8 explicitly sees itself as following on Daniel 7 (see 8:1) and by implication invites us to see it as clarifying some of the allusiveness of that previous vision. Thus the kings to follow the Babylonians are explicitly Median, Persian, and Greek (8:21); the small horn is now indisputably Antiochus Epiphanes, and the crisis which hints at the End is the collection of events which took place in Jerusalem in the 160s.

The kings are now animals fighting each other, animals which thus symbolize national powers full of aggressive strength. The origins of their human power do not come into focus here; there is no indication that it is either demonic or within the purpose of God. The vision reveals not the origin of human power but its destiny.

Horns, and the human strength they symbolize, are strong yet also strangely vulnerable.[3] Each mighty, even apparently unassailable human power is in due course broken by another—sometimes at the height of its achievement, as if the effort involved in that achievement proves too much. God can thus afford to view this process with distanced disdain; the nations will determine their own destinies. The pattern of history is then not one imposed on it by God from outside but one in which the arrogance of power works itself out as one empire arouses the envy of another which challenges and defeats the one which has grown excessively powerful.

The postexilic period as a whole is a period of "wrath" (8:19). It is not one of rebelliousness on Israel's part like the time which led up to the Exile. Yet throughout the postexilic period Israel experiences harshness and affliction, perhaps in that God is still punishing them for the sin that led to the Exile (cf. 9:24?), perhaps simply in that their enemies are treating them with hostility (cf. 11:30 for Antiochus's wrath). Either way, there is a striking contrast between the promise set before people in the sixth century by a prophet such as Zechariah, who implied that the Exile as a time of wrath was about to end (e.g., Zech 1:12–17), and the experience of the postexilic period as Daniel envisions it, where it is not a time of God's comfort but of God's continuing absence.[4]

History as Israel's continuing exile

Daniel 9 begins with Daniel wondering about the fulfillment of a prophecy which Jeremiah uttered just before the fall of Jerusalem (see Jeremiah 29:10). Some people had already been taken into exile, and Jeremiah was writing to urge them to settle down in Babylon—there was going to be no immediate return home. One suspects he sent a copy to the people still living in Jerusalem, who also still needed to take seriously his warnings about God's judgment. The prophecy thus spoke of an exile which would last seventy years before people could return. The point was not a prediction of an exile of seventy rather than sixty-nine or seventy-one years, but a warning that exile would last a normal person's lifetime, so that hardly any who went into exile would return.

In the event, the beginnings of the return from Exile in 537 took place not far from 70 actual years after Judah's submission to Babylon in 605, while the rebuilding of the temple after the Exile (520–516) took place not far from 70 actual years after the final fall of Jerusalem in 587. Thus 2 Chronicles 36:22 and Ezra 1:1 see the events of 537 as the fulfillment of Jeremiah's prophecy, and Zechariah 1:12 and 7:5 imply the same connection with the period of the rebuilding of the temple. Daniel 9, too, pictures Daniel himself wondering about the fulfillment of the prophecy, apparently in 539.

At this point, as at others, however, the message in Daniel's vision relates to events in the 160s. Far from being over within a year or two, as people expected around the time of the fall of Jerusalem, exile and desolation have continued over centuries. While Jews were free to return and rebuild the temple, independence and prosperity never returned to Palestine; indeed, as the events of the second century unfolded, oppression and desolation increased rather than diminished. So how did history and prophecy match? When will God terminate Israel's exile?

The answer comes by setting Jeremiah's prophecy alongside other warnings about exile in Leviticus 26, a chapter which speaks of a sevenfold judgment on sin. In this light, it was quite possible to see why exile should continue way beyond the seventy unkept sabbath years that were due to be exacted (2 Chron 36:21). It could appropriately continue seven times seventy years, or four hundred and ninety years.

Gabriel thus explains to Daniel that actually "seventy sevens have been assigned for your people and for your sacred city" (9:24). Since Jeremiah's seventy years originally denoted not a precise chronological period but rather such a time as would see the passing of virtually everyone who was alive when he spoke, similarly Gabriel would hardly be suggesting 490 years rather than 489 or 491.

That is also implied by the slightly enigmatic nature of the phrase "seventy *sevens*" (the word "years" does not appear).

Indeed, after the symbolic time periods in Daniel 7 and 8 (see chapter 9) we would half-expect another symbolic time measure rather than a chronological one here. So we are not surprised to discover that the figures have to be massaged if Gabriel's prophecy is to be applied to any chronological period of precisely four hundred and ninety years. The figure is a symbolic one, suggesting a period during which God's judgment is exacted in full measure. It lasts much longer than was originally envisaged, but it is not interminable and not out of God's control.

History in its insignificance

Daniel 11 gives the details of secular history more place than any other chapter in Daniel, yet renders history essentially meaningless. The great historian H. A. L. Fisher confessed, "I am unable to find any meaning in history." Shakespeare's Macbeth would agree:

> Tomorrow, and tomorrow, and tomorrow,
> creeps in this petty pace from day to day,
> to the last syllable of recorded time
> . . . a tale
> told by an idiot, full of sound and fury,
> signifying nothing.

It is an attitude toward history very different from that of most Old Testament prophets and psalmists, which we noted at the beginning of chapter 3 above. History unfolds as a pointless sequence of invasions, battles, schemes and frustrations. Military power and political maneuvering are central themes, but military issues are not always settled by the size of an army and political schemes come to nothing. It is a tale of selfishness, irrationality, and chance. Once four great empires contained one another by each terminating the rule of the last. Now two great empires mutually contain each other by frustrating each other's aspirations to wider rule over a period of centuries and thus protect each other from the ultimate arrogance which must provoke God to intervene. Beyond that, neither the hand of justice nor the hand of God is visible in this history. The vision's account matches the experience we often have of history. The history of the postexilic period, like our history, only has meaning as one looks back at it in the light of a revelation of God's purpose which cannot be read off from history itself.

8 THE TIME OF CRISIS

Critical study of the Book of Daniel has sometimes suggested that the whole purpose of the book was to address
the crisis which came about in Jerusalem between 175 and
164 B.C., during the reign of Antiochus Epiphanes. That is
an exaggeration. Daniel 1–6 as a whole lacks any specific
indication that this is the situation which the stories address,
and offers many circumstantial indications that it is not. The
stories' portrait of Nebuchadnezzar and their account of
the possibility of faithful but successful service in the state
hardly suggest that they were created to speak to that
second-century situation. Antiochus is quite different from
Nebuchadnezzar and the experience of Jewish leaders in
their relationship with the state in second-century Jerusalem
was quite different from that of Daniel and his friends
in dispersion. The visions in the second half of the book,
however, do focus with increasing intensity on events in
Jerusalem between 175 and 164.

The attack on the holy ones

The fourth of the fearsome animals in Daniel's first vision (Daniel 7) sprouted ten horns (standing for the kings of the Hellenistic Empires which succeeded the empire of Alexander), and then grew a further small horn which stood for Antiochus. Three of the ten horns are said to be uprooted before this small horn. While the "ten" may possibly be ten particular kings (e.g., those of the Seleucid line), it may more likely be a round figure which should not be pressed.

"Three," however, looks more specific, though interpreters have varied in how they interpret the reference. Perhaps the most likely candidates for the three places are Antiochus's elder brother and predecessor Seleucus IV (for whose violent end Antiochus may have been thought in some way responsible), Seleucus's eldest son Demetrius who was displaced by Antiochus in 175, and Seleucus's younger son, also called Antiochus, who was proclaimed king and acted as co-regent with Antiochus IV for five years but was eventually killed, allegedly at Antiochus's instigation.

We have suggested in the previous chapter that the fourth empire in Daniel 7 is Greece and that the small horn on the animal which represents the Greek Empire is Antiochus Epiphanes, even though the portrait in Daniel 7 in isolation is too allusive actually to require that identification. Many commentators have reckoned that the fourth empire was Rome and that the small horn was thus some Roman figure. But that view depends on taking Daniel 7 in isolation from the rest of the visions, and in particular on assuming that the small horn of Daniel 7 and the small horn of Daniel 8 are different figures.

In fact, they are very similar. In Daniel 7 the small horn behaves in an impressive and humanlike way, comes to look bigger than the others, makes war on holy beings, and prevails over them. The king it represents makes statements hostile to God and plans to change times set by decree, and those times (or perhaps those holy beings) are given into his control for a time limited to "three and a half periods" until his authority is taken away by God's judgment. In Daniel 8 the small horn grows in several directions, attacks the celestial army, and overthrows some of it. It grows within reach of the army commander, attacks the sanctuary itself, and is given control of the daily offerings for a time limited to twenty-three hundred evenings and mornings, until it is broken by supernatural power. The interpretation further emphasizes the king's trickery, power, and destructiveness.

The features of the two accounts of the small horn are thus essentially similar: its size and strength, its partially successful attack on the holy/celestial beings, its interference in God's own realm, and the promise that its power has a limit set to it.

The different images and details in the accounts of the small horn complement each other. In Daniel 8 it grows *from* one of *four* horns instead of *in the midst of ten*: that is, Daniel 8 draws attention to Antiochus's links with the four "parent" post-Alexander kingdoms instead of his links with the long Seleucid and Ptolemaic lines. The differences between the two chapters do not mean that the portraits are at all in conflict. While they *could* denote different kings, juxtaposed in the same book they more naturally denote the same king. Given that the small horn in Daniel 8 is Antiochus, then, this is also the natural understanding of Daniel 7.

It is also the understanding presupposed by the oldest allusion to Daniel 7, in a section of the Jewish work called the Sibylline Oracles which comes from a period not long after Antiochus. It is also presupposed by 2 Esdras, a later Jewish work from after the fall of Jerusalem in A.D. 70. In 2 Esdras 12:10-12 God explains to "Ezra," "the eagle you saw rising from the sea represents the fourth kingdom in the vision seen by your brother Daniel. But he was not given the interpretation which I am now giving you. . . ." Then God goes on to describe the Romans. 2 Esdras is explicit, then, that the understanding of the fourth empire as the Romans was not Daniel's own but a later, inspired reinterpretation of the vision's original meaning. It is this reinterpretation which is presupposed in the New Testament. But it is overtly a reinterpretation of the vision's original meaning.

The fourth animal's small horn has features which mark it as more than merely animal. It looks like a human being and speaks impressively (7:8). In due course it will become clear that these are the looks and words of covetousness with regard to worldly power and arrogance before God (7:20, 25).

Antiochus's attempt "to change times set by decree" (7:25) are often reckoned to involve the imposition of a new calendar (a 360-day lunar calendar to replace the 364-day solar one). Such issues were of great importance in certain circles during the second century, but the more detailed accounts of Antiochus's interfering with Jewish religious matters of which we read in succeeding chapters do not refer to changes in the calendar. Conversely it would be strange for Daniel 7 to single out one such feature of Antiochus's policy. More likely "changing the times" has the same meaning as it had earlier (2:21): it refers to deciding how history unfolds and how one regime follows another. These things are fixed by God's decree. In forcing his way to the throne and bull-dozing his way through history Antiochus has defied God's shaping of history and taken the helm of history for himself.

The desolating rebellion

We have seen that Daniel 8 views the postexilic period as a whole as a period of wrath. It draws towards its close with Antiochus, as the story of the four Hellenistic empires itself draws to a close (8:19, 23). Antiochus is portrayed as a person of ruthless boldness and artful cleverness (8:23-25). These are not mere randomly observed aspects of a particular person's character, but key elements in the standard portrayal of a wicked tyrant. He fulfills all that people dreaded of the ultimate despot.

Antiochus is described both as attacking the heavenly powers and as interfering with the worship of the earthly sanctuary, halting the system of regular offerings and suspending the authority of the Torah over Israel (8:10-12). These two acts are not independent or separate events: an attack on the Jerusalem temple, on the Israelite people, and on the priesthood is implicitly an attack on the God who is worshiped there and on his supernatural associates who identify with Israel.

Antiochus's actual cultic innovation is described as "the desolating rebellion" (8:13); the similar expression "desolating abomination" appears in later visions (9:27; 11:31; 12:11). These terms apparently parody the name of the god *Ba'al Shamem*, "Lord of heaven," whose worship Antiochus introduced into the temple. Antiochus perhaps believed that he could be identified with the God the Jews worshipped. "Rebellion" or "abomination" replaces *Ba'al*, indicating a theological evaluation of Antiochus's religious innovation— it is an act of rebellion against the true God, an act of monstrous sacrilege. "Desolating" (*shomem*) replaces "heaven" (*shamem*) because both words have the same letters, though they are pronounced differently. Again the replacement word offers a judgment of Antiochus's actions. He brings desolation to city and sanctuary (see 8:24, 25; 9:26).

Daniel does not give a straightforward, literal description of what Antiochus actually introduced into the temple. It has often been understood as an image of the god (or of Antiochus himself), but the account in 1 Maccabees 1 points rather to a rebuilding of the actual altar to serve its new god.

Either way, the rebelliousness which preoccupies Daniel's visions is not Israel's but the nations'. It is a rebelliousness which "reaches full measure" with Antiochus (cf. 8:23): the image suggests that God is forbearing with the sin of gentiles, but that this involves allowing their sin to reach an extreme form which then necessitates a radical punishment which will also mean deliverance and blessing for Israel (cf. Genesis 15:16).

Jesus and Paul take up the motif of rebels reaching full measure and apply it to the Jewish people, in the light of their refusal to recognize Jesus (Matt 23:32; 1 Thess 2:16). Presumably, the motif's openness to being reapplied that way means it can be reapplied again to the Church if it turns its back on God's way (cf. Rom 11:17-22). As well as being a call to loyalty under persecution, Daniel's vision is thus also a call to humility and repentance on the part of people not under persecution.

The seventieth seven

Israel's continuing exile reaches its lowest point in the events from 171-164 (seven chronological years!); but this will also be the time which sees its termination.

Some specific indication of the events of this last "seven" appears in Gabriel's closing words (9:26, 27). It is a time of devastation, battle, and desolation: such is the seriousness of the trouble brought to people, city, and temple by the combined forces of heathen ruler(s) and usurper priest(s).

The terms used to describe these events show that this crisis is seen as an anticipatory embodiment of the last great battle, a historical embodiment of the first great battle between the forces of chaos and the forces of order. Specifically, Gabriel speaks of an anointed being cut off (presumably the high priest Onias III, displaced in 175 and killed in 171). His losing city and sanctuary sounds like a reference to Onias's displacement and withdrawal for safety to Daphne, near Antioch, where he was eventually killed; it is this event which marks the beginning of the last seven years of trouble. The "leader to come" who follows Onias is then Jason, who succeeded him as high priest and both corrupted and devastated the people of Jerusalem.

The passage highlights the trouble brought to faithful Jews by fellow-Jews whom they saw as collaborating with gentile oppressors as well as by these oppressors themselves. It is probably this unholy alliance between reformist Jews and Antiochus that is the "covenant" which "prevails for the multitude"—virtually meaning "prevails against them," the multitude being the main body of Jews who wanted to remain loyal to the Torah.

Halfway through the final "seven" during which this alliance is operative, the regular worship of the temple is suspended and Antiochus's repellant alternative is imposed, as Daniel 8 has already described. The desolating abomination appears "on a wing"—more likely indicating something Antiochus put on the altar with its winglike corners than something he put on the temple roof with its winglike "pinnacles." Devastation of this kind must continue to overwhelm desolate Jerusalem until what God has decreed is exhausted.

The king who asserts himself

Daniel's last vision covers once again the same ground as the previous ones, but does so at each point in more detail. It tells us more about the detail of events in the history of the Middle East under the Hellenistic kings, more about the suffering of the Jews in the 160s, and more about their vindication at the End.

In chapter 1 we have noted the outline of Antiochus's involvement with the Jews as Daniel 11 relates it. From the beginning (11:21) the account implies a value judgment regarding Antiochus, a man whom no one would initially take any account of because he had no right to the throne, but who carved a way to power with consummate ease by skillful diplomacy. From the beginning, too, the account puts its focus on his extraordinary military achievements in his relationship with Egypt, his intervention in matters which Jews saw as religious but which Antiochus will have seen as matters of state, and his success in winning the allegiance of certain groups in Judea. These were people who in return for a share in the exercise of power in internal Jewish affairs would cooperate with his policies and should be capable of ensuring that those policies were actually implemented in Jerusalem.

The evaluation becomes most overt with 11:36–39. As in other chapters, Antiochus is assumed to be attacking not merely a people and its religion but God. He acts as he pleases (and that standard description of apparently unchallengeable authority is one that regularly presages unexpected disaster). He exalts himself and magnifies himself. The verbs are ones only used in the Bible of God on the one hand, and on the other of human beings who impiously assert themselves against God and have judgment declared on them. Antiochus proclaimed himself Antiochus IV Epiphanes, "[God] Manifest," used the title "God" on coins, applied symbols of deity to himself, plundered temples, and intervened in religious matters in his realm.

None of this was peculiar to him; like leaders everywhere, Hellenistic kings regularly associated themselves closely with religion in various ways, to support their position. If Antiochus took his divinity more seriously than most, as some scholars have thought, the reason may have been as political as the considerations that shaped other aspects of his policies. It helped to bind his empire together and to bind it to him. For Antiochus, as for other kings, religion was—among other things—the servant of his political position.

"The god of his fathers" and "the god women love" (11:37) are probably key gods of the northern and southern realms. The former would have been Apollo, whom Antiochus replaced with Zeus as *the* god of the Seleucid dynasty, to provide religious support for the irregularity involved in his becoming king. It is Zeus who is subsequently described as the "stronghold god" (11:38, 39), as he was the god worshiped as *Ba'al Shamem* by the Syrian garrison in Jerusalem. "The god women love" would then have been a god specially favored in Egypt, Adonis or Dionysus, who was slighted by Antiochus's various encroachments on the southern kingdom. It was not only in his dealings with Jews that Antiochus subordinated religion to politics. It seems likely that early in Antiochus's reign, either on Antiochus's initiative or on that of reformist Jews, the constitutional position of Jerusalem was changed. It ceased to be the center of a community governing itself in accordance with its own laws (the Torah) and became a Hellenistic city-state like others by which Antiochus controlled his empire. Its citizenship would then comprise those who accepted a Hellenistic way of life. Reformist Jews might be able to see this as involving no compromise over essential tenets of Jewish faith, but conservative Jews would view it as abandonment of the Torah and of the terms Yahweh had set for Israel's covenant relationship, which excluded covenants with other peoples.

The developments in Antiochus's policies noted in chapter 1 eventually led, however, to the suspension of regular Jewish worship and the setting up of the "desolating abomination" already discussed in connection with Daniel 8 and 9. It seems that Jews who had been able to accept the establishment of a Hellenistic community now found themselves drawn into cooperation with a policy that no doubt went beyond their original expectations or desires. To Jews who had rejected such developments from the beginning, the abominations of Antiochus were a provocation to which God had to respond. They heralded the End.

9 THE END

At the time when Nebuchadnezzar had his first dream, Daniel was able to tell him that his thoughts "concerned what is to happen in the future" (2:29): he was wondering how events would unfold over coming years and even after his own day. Nebuchadnezzar himself perhaps remembered as much about the night of his dream, even if he could not remember the dream's content, and he had that much check on purported reconstructions and interpretations of his dream. Daniel was also able to tell him that his dream related to "the end of the era" (2:28); Nebuchadnezzar may not have known that.

"The end of the era" is literally "the end of the days," a phrase that comes fourteen times in the Old Testament. The word for "end" denotes not a single moment (Hebrew and Aramaic have other words with that meaning), but the last part or the aftermath of something. "The days" are a period which may be long but will not be interminable, a period which will or must elapse before certain predictions, promises, or warnings come true. "The end of the days" is thus the time of the fulfillment of these promises or warnings. This fulfillment may come at the End of the Age, but of itself "the end of the days" does not have an eschatological meaning. It only acquires this association through being used in contexts which refer to the End.

So Daniel points us toward a special significance attaching to the last part of Nebuchadnezzar's dream. It thus introduces a feature which we have noted in a number of the visions: they presuppose a setting in the Exile, but look beyond that to events in some generations' time which will bring history to its climax.

The rock hewn from a crag and the rule of God

The fourth regime pictured by Nebuchadnezzar's dream has a crushing power but an unexpected fragility, which it cannot mend in a lasting way (2:40–43). Whatever the identity of this regime, its significance is to reveal that the imperial colossus will not stand for ever. It will be replaced not by a fifth regime but by a quite different sovereignty (v 44).

There is no suggestion that it is Israel that exercises this rule; the sovereignty is God's own, apparently directly exercised by God. The vision's promise concerning the End is that God's rule of the world (often symbolized in the Old Testament in terms of a mountain: see e.g., Isaiah 2:2, 3) will then at last become reality. This will only come about by the act of God; in that sense it is heavenly and supernatural. But it will come about on earth, not merely in heaven. God will change the Lordship of this world, but not abandon this world. The qualities of its new rule are not defined except by saying that it is God's and that it lasts, both qualities which contrast with those of its predecessors.

The humanlike figure and the rule of a holy people

In the further vision of four regimes in Daniel 7, the last is again a powerful and violent one, particularly when headed by its final king, a man of arrogant spirit and persecuting tendency. At the height of his achievement, however, God's court sits and declares judgment on him (7:11).

This follows a person's taking his seat on a throne (7:9, 10). He is someone advanced in years and thus august and venerable, judicious and wise, and someone of bright, luminous appearance and thus of splendor and nobility. Indeed, the flames and fire and the myriad attendants hint that he is more than a mere human being, though in other respects he is human in appearance. There is no indication that the location has changed since the description of the previous verses; the events apparently take place on earth. As at the royal court, books of record (such as decisions the king has made, obligations he has imposed, and policy he has determined) are consulted.

Our attention is then directed to the heavens, from where descends a second figure, to be presented at court (7:13). The expression used to describe him has been literalistically rendered "a son of man," but this misses the fact that the Aramaic phrase is a relatively ordinary one meaning "a human being." It has the word "like" in front of it, in the manner of the animals referred to in 7:4–6 and the supernatural figures in 8:15 and 10:16, 18, so we might translate it "something like a human being" or "one in human likeness." The word "like" adds a note of mystery to the visions.

To describe the figure as humanlike does not indicate whether he is actually human (any more than is the case with the one advanced in years, who stands for God); the parallel with those other supernatural figures might indicate he stands for a heavenly being. His human appearance indicates a contrast between him and the animals. Human status was granted to the first animal and grasped after by the small horn; it suggests being in a position of authority in the world. Thus this humanlike figure is fittingly invested as king (7:14). He is given a sovereignty on earth like God's own, one which replaces that of the entities symbolized by the animals.

What does the vision refer to? It is clear enough that the one advanced in years stands for God. But even the explanatory part of the vision is rather reticent concerning who the humanlike figure stands for. Verse 18 tells us that "holy ones on high will acquire the kingship," without quite saying that the humanlike figure actually represents them and without telling us who the holy ones themselves are.

"Holy" in the Old Testament is not essentially a moral term; it denotes the distinctive, absolute transcendence of God rather than God's moral nature. The term "holy" is then by extension applied to other supernatural beings, to earthly entities associated with deity such as shrines and their personnel, to Israel as a people distinctively set apart by God, and to people within Israel who do actually realize the vocation to be distinctively God's. So here the "holy ones" who are symbolized by the humanlike figure and who receive the kingship could be supernatural beings, or Israel as a whole, or the priesthood, or a group of the faithful within Israel. "On high," too, could refer to Israelites or to supernatural beings, though the term is more often used in the latter connection.

The supernatural overtones of "humanlike figure" and "holy ones on high" suggest that these figures cannot stand simply for that down-to-earth Israel to which visionary and audience belong. The humanlike figure and the holy ones more likely stand for supernatural entities who take over authority in the world on God's behalf. On the other hand, if the figures do stand for heavenly beings, these will probably be ones associated with Israel in some way, like Michael in Daniel 10-12. They are not merely a supernatural people quite separate from Israel.

But the allusiveness of these elements in the vision needs to be honored. Daniel parallels other biblical prophecies, which regularly become symbolic and allusive when they move from portraying current history to portraying the ultimate fulfillment of God's purpose. So Daniel affirms that the worldly kingdoms will be replaced by God's rule; he does not make explicit how. The ultimate events and realities to come cannot be described straightforwardly like the kingdoms the beasts represent.[1]

The humanlike figure and the holy ones take no active role in the drama. The humanlike figure is simply invested, without his acting or striving. Nor do the holy ones fight— at least, not successfully. It is their suffering that brings their attacker's downfall. One is reminded of God's disarming principalities and powers through Christ's being crucified (Col 2:15).

The promise of the End in Daniel 7, then, presupposes a situation in which a wicked power crushes the world, vaunts itself against God, oppresses those who belong to God, and tries to turn the helm of history its own way (7:23-25). This goes on for a period of time, then for double that. Its self-assertiveness seems capable of continuing for much longer, perhaps for double that time again, so that it lasts seven periods altogether—in effect for an eternity (it seems unlikely that the periods referred to in 7:25 can be directly translated into chronological lengths of time). Just as that seemed possible, Calvin notes,

> God then began to seat himself, as he had previously appeared to be passive, and not to exercise justice in the world. For when things are disturbed and mingled with

much darkness, who can say, "God reigns"? God seems to be shut up in heaven, when things are discomposed and turbulent upon earth. On the other hand, he is said to ascend his tribunal when he assumes to himself the office of a judge, and openly demonstrates that he is neither asleep nor absent, though he has hid from human perception.[2]

The freedom of the sanctuary

In the context of the more specific (though still symbolic) account of events in the 160s which comes in Daniel 8, again the question arises, "How long will this be allowed to last?" The cry of the holy ones takes up the cry of afflicted Israel, often expressed in lament psalms. The response to the cry is "two thousand three hundred days," after which the sanctuary will "emerge in the right" or be vindicated (8:13, 14). Perhaps the two thousand three hundred days should be connected with a period such as the one which lasted from the removal of the high priest in 171 to the rededication of the sanctuary in 164, or that which lasted from the cessation of sacrifice in 167 to the victory of Judas the Maccabee in 160 (see 1 Maccabees 7). But the three and a half periods of time in 7:25 have a symbolic rather than a literally chronological significance, as do the seventy "sevens" of 9:24–27; there is some evidence that twenty-three is also a symbolic number in postexilic writings, so we may be mistaken in trying to connect two thousand three hundred days with a particular period of literally that chronological length.

Whatever the precise reference of the two thousand three hundred days, the vision promises that the period of affliction will not go on for ever. God has set the moment for it to come to an end (8:19). Antiochus will mysteriously fall (8:25). His end is not merely the fruit of historical forces, like the passing of power from one empire to another at earlier stages. Even if the historical forces which bring the downfall of evil can be traced, there is something supernatural to it, as there was something demonic about Antiochus's actions, and as heaven itself was hurt by his attacks on the people of God and the sanctuary of God.

The end of his horrendous affliction will also be *the* End (8:17). It can be identified with the closing scene of the history of Israel and the nations (2:28) and the moment of a final judgment (7:26). Yet it is not an end which means that human history comes to a stop. By speaking of the restoration of the sanctuary as earlier chapters have spoken of a new kingship on earth (2:44; 7:14,18,27), the vision takes for granted that human history on earth will continue.

The end of Israel's exile

As we noted in discussing the book's portrayal of post-exilic history, Daniel 9 sees this history as a prolonging of the Exile. The experience of desolation continues as God continues to exact judgment on Israel for the sins which led to the fall of Jerusalem. The "End" in Daniel 9 is thus the end of that exile. The affirmation that exile will last for seventy years, or even seventy sevens [of years], becomes a promise that exile will therefore have a term to it. An end will come.

Gabriel's opening words already advertise that Israel's exile will not be merely endless and pointless trouble. The seventy sevens are designed to achieve something. Indeed, Gabriel tells Daniel, by the end of the seventy sevens six things will have been achieved "for your people and for your sacred city" (9:24). Those words indicate that the concern of the promise is Israel and Jerusalem. It does not have a world-wide perspective (except insofar as all that God does with Israel affects the destiny of the whole world). As in previous chapters, the writer is not speaking of the end of all history;

and when sin is referred to it is that of Israel and her post-exilic oppressors, not the sin of all the world.

Gabriel speaks first of three negative achievements: "to end the rebellion, to do away with failures, to wipe away waywardness." The three expressions are approximately synonymous. Wickedness is being characterized as rebellion against God's authority, failure to achieve God's standards, and wandering from the way God prescribes. It may be that the promise that wickedness will be brought to an end applies both to Israel's wickedness, a central theme in the prayer which precedes this promise (9:4–19), and to Antiochus's wickedness, more commonly the theme in these chapters. But here the agency or the subject of wrongdoing is not in focus. Gabriel is concerned with the objective result of that wrongdoing, the sacrilege in the sanctuary which he promises will be rectified.

Three positives correspond to the three negatives: the seventy sevens have been assigned "to bring in lasting vindication, to seal a prophet's vision, to anoint a most sacred place." The vindication will be the vindication of the sanctuary, already referred to in 8:14 where the related verb has been used. The desecration of the sanctuary has cast a slur on it, which will now be removed. The prophetic vision which will thus be sealed will be the prophecy of Jeremiah with which the chapter begins and ends; it will be fulfilled and thus confirmed by God's act of salvation. The anointing of a most sacred place will be the act which effects the reconsecration of the sanctuary after it had been defiled by Antiochus; the expression here is the one used in connection with the original consecration of the sanctuary (see e.g., Exodus 30:26–29).

The climax of wrath and the promise of life

Daniel's last vision affirms that the "End" is indeed coming (11:27, 35, 40, 45; 12:4, 6, 9, 13)—the word underlines the punctiliar, definitive fact and finality of the reversal God promises. But events must always await the "set time" (11:27, 29, 35; 12:7): God is in control and God's purpose is at work even in the abominations and the afflictions of the Antiochene period, preventing the king from fulfilling all his own purposes. It is a time of wrath (11:36), a time of unprecedented trouble (12:1), a time of awesome events (12:6); but the idea of wrath being "complete" (11:36) implies that it cannot go on without limit.

At a recognizable moment (11:40) the prophecy moves from depiction of actual historical events to a visionary scenario of judgment and redemption. The End actually arrives. This has led some readers to assume that at this point in Daniel 11 (or at some earlier point in the chapter) the vision ceases referring to Antiochus and from now on concerns the Antichrist. But there is no hint in Daniel 11 of such a change. On the contrary, verse 40 declares that "the southern king will engage in a struggle with *him*," and the "him" must be the northern king of previous verses, Antiochus.

There is indeed a sense in which Antiochus himself is a demonic figure, as there is a sense in which the people he attacks are a heavenly people. Yet Antiochus was not literally fighting angels; rather, that was the significance of his attacking people and sanctuary (see 8:10–12). The visible realities such as the Jewish people and the Jerusalem temple had a transcendent significance which Antiochus denied. Heaven and earth are not two separate, discontinuous, disconnected worlds. Each underlies the other. So also Antiochus is an embodiment of demonic pretension, but Daniel is not referring to there being an independently existent supernatural being separate from Antiochus who is using him or is foreshadowed by him. Rather the fact that Antiochus is an embodiment of godless wickedness means that the language used of him could be used of the Antichrist or Satan, and a passage like this one can help us to understand something of the significance of the Antichrist or Satan even though it was not originally written about them.

The pagan scholar Porphyry (some of whose work on Daniel is known to us through quotations in a commentary by the church father Jerome) inferred that verses 40–45 describe how Antiochus actually died, but the trouble is they do not. The portrayal does not correspond to what actually happened. 1 and 2 Maccabees give different accounts of his death, but they agree that it took place (at the end of 164) in the course of a not-wholly-successful campaign in Persia.

Now we are familiar with the fact that biblical prophecy does not generally give a literal advance portrayal of events; Old Testament prophecies of the Messiah such as Isaiah 9:2–7 are not literal pictures of Jesus. They are portraits painted in the light of Scriptures that people knew already, promises that those Scriptures would come true. But they do not give a basis for working out precisely how God will bring about salvation or judgment. We could not have predicted the precise nature of Jesus' ministry from the prophecies that are fulfilled in him—it is only in retrospect that people were able to see him prophesied there.

As we have hinted in chapter 4 above, similarly the portrayal of the northern king's end in Daniel 11:40–45 is not shaped by the nature of the bare events themselves, as they would turn out historically, as if Gabriel was offering a literal preview of these. It is shaped as a whole as well as in its detail by the Old Testament theme of the attack of a gentile foe who is defeated and killed near the gates of Jerusalem (e.g., Psalms 2; 46; 48; 76), a theme already reworked in prophetic passages such as Isaiah 10; 14:24, 25; 31; Ezekiel 38, 39; Joel 2:20; Zechariah 14, as well as by the prophetic portrayals of judgment on Egypt (Isa 19; Jer 43:8–13; 46; Ezek 29–32). So the portrait is not a failed attempt to give a literal account of how matters will end, but a reliable promise that God's Word will be fulfilled.

The seer thus imagines Antiochus's deeds reaching even beyond anything we have read of already. He attempts at last to win the ultimate victory over the southern king. In the course of doing so, he recapitulates Nebuchadnezzar's invasion, sparing Israel's old enemies who had been in a position to take advantage over Israel then. He goes on to fulfill the prophecies that envisaged Nebuchadnezzar's final defeat of Egypt itself. But the moment of triumph again heralds downfall. The final battle takes place near the gates of Jerusalem, as it must, but the one who had schemed against an unsuspecting and vulnerable people finds himself God's victim.[3]

The medieval scholars who divided the Bible into chapters introduced a chapter division at this point, but the text itself continues without a break. It continues to relate what will happen "at that time" (12:1)—the time of which the previous verses had spoken in describing the last great battle, involving Antiochus. There is no hint that Gabriel is referring to some far future moment. Rather he continues to speak of the unprecedented "time of trouble" which Antiochus brought to the Jewish people as he sought to terminate the worship of the true God and to annihilate God's people. Gabriel now reveals the supernatural event which lies behind Antiochus's defeat.

Michael, Israel's representative in heaven, arises in the heavenly court on Israel's behalf to point out that their names can be found written in the Book, the citizen list of the true Jerusalem. They have no business to be thrust precipitously into the realm of death. It is Michael's victory at this point over Antiochus's heavenly representative that means Antiochus is defeated on earth and that Daniel's people "escape": perhaps from dying, perhaps from the realm of the dead. Certainly Gabriel goes on to speak of many who have died coming back to life: He may refer to people who died during the Antiochene crisis even though they maintained their faithfulness to God, or may have in mind the bulk of faithful Jews (those who were martyred and those who were not). They will be vindicated; their faithful leaders will receive great honor to reverse the shame of their humiliation and death (12:3). People who were not faithful yet seemed to triumph will also awake, but for condemnation.

In these verses Gabriel continues to portray the future on the basis of Scripture; the vision's imaginative portrayal is not an attempt at literal prediction. Further, Gabriel is continuing to promise a solution to a specific historical problem. He is not offering a piece of systematically formulated theological teaching but a comforting vision. The oppressive reign of Antiochus will not last forever. The one who epitomized godlessness will fall. The people who resist him will be vindicated. Those for whom that vindication comes too late will be brought back to life to resume the life they had lost, while those who led them in the way of faithfulness will shine like stars. It is a picture way of affirming that God will see that truth, commitment, and faithfulness will be vindicated. The martyrs will not lose their share in the life, glory, joy, and fellowship of the people of God (no individualistic vision of resurrection, this). And in fulfillment of Gabriel's words, Antiochus and his supporters have not been forgotten, like most of the dead. Wherever the gospel of Daniel has been preached through the whole world, what these men did has been spoken of and their memory perpetuated.

It is striking that other peoples began to hope for new life after death long before the Jews. Perhaps God wanted Israel to learn to take this life really seriously and not indulge in pie-in-the-sky beliefs. The grounds for the affirmation that Daniel now makes perhaps lie for him in the nature of God as the One who is faithful to oppressed Israel. But as the earlier history of God's dealings with Israel shaped the way the Book of Daniel saw events in the second century, so Daniel's vision of the awakening and vindication of the holy and discerning martyr shaped the way Jesus and his followers understood *him*. It was the death and resurrection of Jesus that more than any other event brought the End into history, so that by a feedback process, that Christ event is the vindication of Daniel's vision.

Once again Daniel wishes to know how long the time of suffering will be, and (in words similar to the ones which appear in 7:25) he is told that it will last three and a half "set periods." Like us, Daniel finds this more puzzling than illuminating, tries asking the question again, and is given a further answer in terms of a number of days—1290 and 1335 (12:11, 12). The figures probably have some significance in connection with the calendar.

As we noted in chapter 8, various calendars were in use in the second century, and the question of the right calendar was a topic of dispute. The Babylonians used a lunar calendar with a year of 354 days, the Essenes a solar calendar with a year of 364 days, the Hellenistic regimes a lunar-solar calendar with a year of 360 days. In each case the calendar was corrected to the true length of the solar year, just over 365 days, by intercalating months.

Daniel's periods of days can be related to all three calendars and to several sets of events in the 160s: that is, each could cover the time from one or other of Antiochus's edicts or its enforcement to one or other of the events that marked the effective end of the period of oppression.

When comes the End? The New Testament and after

So, the abominations and the afflictions of Antiochus, and the judgment and deliverance God brought in response to them, were the "End." In what sense?

Daniel's vision of the ultimate establishment of God's rule was not fulfilled in the historical periods to which the book refers, the Babylonian, the Persian, or the Greek. In this it parallels many prophetic oracles in the Old Testament. These gave the impression that the Day of Yahweh was about to dawn, but after them things continue as they have before. That happens again when Christ comes and speaks of the imminent establishing of God's rule (see 2 Peter 3:4).

Yet each prophet's words were received as from God, even though they did not seem to have come true. This was partly because people believed that they *would* find their fulfillment in time, partly because they knew that they *had* seen some measure of fulfillment already—hence the conviction that further fulfillment would also follow.

So it is also with Daniel's visions. The book itself has to handle the fact that promises of the ultimate realization of God's kingship have not been fulfilled. It does this, not by turning that kingship into something nationalistic (Yahweh is [to be] Israel's king) or individualistic (Yahweh's kingship is [to be] realized in the believer's personal life) or otherworldly (Yahweh's kingship is [to be] realized in heaven) or humanly-generated (we are responsible for bringing in Yahweh's kingship). It reaffirms a vision of a universal, corporate, this-worldly, God-given reign of God. But it does that in the light of the conviction that this vision does find some partial realizations now. The empires that Daniel and his readers knew *did* disappear; the rule of the God of heaven *was* reestablished in Jerusalem.

There are no pointers in Daniel's visions toward a personal messiah's being integral to the final establishment of God's rule, though when Jews of the first century A.D. heard the man Jesus of Nazareth proclaim that God's rule was now arriving, they saw him doing things that in themselves suggested the rule of God brought into their midst. The reign which is at hand is the one which Daniel promised (2:44; 7:22). The time he spoke of is fulfilled. Jesus' virgin birth makes a parallel point to the picture of the rock breaking off without human involvement (2:34).[4] Jesus speaks of himself as the stone that crushes, the very embodiment of the rule of God (Luke 20:18; cf. Daniel 2:44, 45).

Luke actually opens his Gospel with Gabriel again appearing at the time of the evening offering, as in Daniel 9. That begins a chain of events that lead via the birth of Jesus to his being presented in the temple, a chain of events that take 490 days to unfold—another fulfillment of the seventy sevens of which Gabriel spoke. (The New Testament does not link the Christ event with a period of 490 years ending with Christ's death.)

The "humanlike figure" of Daniel 7 provided a key image by which Jesus describes himself in the Gospels. In Daniel it is an ordinary expression which in the context does not denote a specific individual, still less a messianic figure. But by New Testament times, the expression had come to suggest an individual "son of man"—that phrase is a literalistic translation of the Aramaic expression, as strange an expression in the Greek of the New Testament as it is in English. The Gospels declare that Jesus is "that Son of man" who "has authority on earth" (Mark 2:10; cf. Matthew 28:18). They thus use Daniel 7 to express the conviction that *Jesus* (not any other alleged messiah or hero) has ascended as "Son of man" and will return with the clouds.

Jesus and the Gospel writers had apparently also noted that Daniel 7 speaks of the suffering of the holy ones. On the basis of the fact that the "Son of man" stands for the holy ones, they can also connect with Daniel 7 their awareness that "the Son of man must suffer" (Mark 8:31) before he "comes in glory" (Mark 8:38) "with the clouds of heaven" (Mark 14:62). Further, Jesus qualifies the statement that the Son of man came to be served (Dan 7:14) by declaring that he comes first to serve (Mark 10:45). It is in keeping with this affirmation that in Revelation the King among kings is also the lamb with the marks of slaughter upon him (Rev 5:6; 17:14), which excludes any triumphalist understanding of his kingship.[5]

A Christian who lives much later than New Testament times has to face other questions regarding the claim that Jesus brings about the rule of God in the world. That rule of God continues to be more an object of hope than of sight. We still pray, "may your rule come" (Luke 11:2). Precisely at moments when such a vision is difficult to believe, Daniel's readers are urged to take it with utmost seriousness (2:45; 8:26; 10:21).

And when the New Testament seeks to describe the End still to come, it again utilizes the way Daniel speaks of the future—just as the Book of Daniel itself had reused prophetic material from books such as Isaiah. Jesus' discourse concerning the End (Mark 13) speaks in Danielic fashion of troubling rumors, the final affliction, many stumbling, the need to endure to the end, the deliverance of the elect, the desolating sacrilege, the need to understand, and the coming of the Son of man in clouds with great power and glory.

The same way of speaking influences the way Paul speaks of the End in terms of people rising and of those who are still alive being caught up with them in the clouds (1 Thess 4, 5). The account of the resurrection in 1 Corinthians 15 is also shaped by Daniel 7, while Paul's portrait of the lawless man in 2 Thessalonians 2 reflects the portrait of Antiochus in Daniel. But no New Testament document is more thoroughly permeated with Old Testament phraseology and images than Revelation, and no Old Testament book influences Revelation more than Daniel—a book which had been written for a community under analogous pressure to that which affected the audience of Revelation.

In particular, John's opening vision of Christ and of heaven (Rev 1, 4, 5) is shaped in part by Daniel 7 and also by the description of the angelic appearance in Daniel 10, while the animals in Daniel 7 are an important source for the vision of the animal in Revelation 13 and 17.

Interpreters have argued hard and long over the identity of the four kingdoms in Daniel's visions and how they relate to empires after Daniel's own day and into our own. But in a sense, such arguments miss the point. For the recipients of the book, what mattered was that they lived under the fourth regime, and when successive generations have re-applied the scheme of empires to their own day, in principle they have responded to the vision in the way it sought. Whether the mighty empire that controls their destiny is Rome or Turkey or Islam or Britain or America or Israel or Russia, the vision still applies. The very use of symbolism in these visions encourages their reapplication to later embodiments of the same dark forces as those of Daniel's day. Even in his interpretations of the visions Daniel does not say who they refer to, and thus he leaves the text open to being reapplied as international history continues to be a process in which one people after another dominates the world and seeks to make itself God.

The cosmic significance which Daniel's visions attach to Antiochus becomes especially illuminating in the nuclear age. Humanity now has the power to destroy itself and the world in which it lives. There is something utterly unprecedented about this situation, and something theologically quite novel. God has allowed humanity to discover how to bring to an end the story which it did not begin. What is extravagance in Daniel's visions is now reality. Daniel looks in the face the possibility of human power and arrogance toppling the rule of heaven over the world. It affirms that the powers of heaven may be assailed and hurt, but that God will still reserve the last word.

The implication is not that human efforts for peace are unnecessary. The Daniel whose visions we are considering is the man of political commitment and religious faithfulness of

103

whom we read in the stories about him. To say that human peace-seeking is unnecessary if peace must be God's achievement is like saying that seeking righteousness is unnecessary if our relationship with God must be God's gift (Romans 6:1). Paul's response to that inference is not to qualify his affirmation that everything depends on grace; it is to recall the objector to the fact that righteousness is an end, not a means. Similarly we seek peace because it is the godlike thing to do, not because God is necessarily dependent on our doing so. And as we do so, God may well choose to utilize our peace-seeking in bringing peace about. It is possible to speed the coming of the day of God (2 Pet 3:12)—or to delay it.

NOTES

Chapter 2 Faithfulness—Divine and Human

1. N. W. Porteous, *Daniel* (London/Philadelphia: SCM/Westminster, 1965; rev. ed. 1979).

2. W. Wink, *Naming the Powers* (Philadelphia: Fortress, 1984), 110-11.

3. A. Lacocque, *The Book of Daniel*, trans. D. Pellauer (London/Atlanta: SPCK/Knox, 1979).

4. Augustine, Sermon xxxii 15 on Psalm 15, as quoted by E. Bickerman, *The God of the Maccabees* (Leiden: Brill, 1979), v.

Chapter 3 Sovereignty—Divine and Human

1. So J. Moltmann, *Theology of Hope* (London/New York: SCM/Harper, 1967), 133-34.

2. A. Bentzen, *Daniel* (Tübingen: Mohr, 1937; 2d ed. 1952).

3. D. Aukerman, *Darkening Valley* (New York: Seabury, 1981), 50-51.

4. See the comments of Theodoret in his commentary, published in *Patrologia Graeca* 81:1255-1546.

5. A. Lacocque, *The Book of Daniel*, trans. D. Pellauer (London/Atlanta: SPCK/Knox, 1979).

6. J. J. Collins, *Daniel* (Grand Rapids: Eerdmans, 1984), on the chapter.

7. Aukerman, 102–08.

8. R. S. Wallace, *The Lord Is King: The Message of Daniel* (Leicester/Downers Grove, Ill.: IVP, 1979), on 3:8–12.

9. J. G. Baldwin, *Daniel* (Leicester/Grand Rapids: IVP/ Eerdmans, 1978).

10. W. S. Towner, *Daniel* (Atlanta: Knox, 1984).

11. W. Wink, *Naming the Powers* (Philadelphia: Fortress, 1984), 111.

12. Towner, *Daniel.*

Chapter 4   Insight—Divine and Human

1. So E. L. Ehrlich, *Der Traum im Alten Testament* (Berlin: Töpelmann, 1953), 92.

2. J. Boehmer, *Reich Gottes und Menschensohn im Buch Daniel* (Leipzig: Hinrichs, 1899), 62–63.

3. From *Ancient Near East Texts*, ed. J. B. Pritchard (Princeton: Princeton University Press, revised 1969), 606; cf. *Near Eastern Religious Texts Relating to the Old Testament*, ed. W. Beyerlin (London/ Philadelphia: SCM/Westminster, 1978), 118–22.

4. H. Kosmala, *Studies, Essays, and Reviews* (Leiden: Brill, 1978), 1:149–53.

5. W. S. Towner, *Daniel* (Atlanta: Knox, 1984), on the passage.

Chapter 5   Daniel's God and Daniel's Prayer

1. J. Calvin, *Commentaries on the Book of the Prophet Daniel,* 2 vols. (Edinburgh: CTS, 1852–53), on the passage.

2. W. Wink, *Unmasking the Powers* (Philadelphia: Fortress, 1986), 91.

3. J. Scharbert in *Theological Dictionary of the Old Testament,* eds. G. J. Botterweck and H. Ringgren (Grand Rapids: Eerdmans, 1975), II:293.

4. G. von Rad, *Old Testament Theology*, vol. 1 (Edinburgh/ New York: Oliver and Boyd/Harper, 1962), 342–43, 357–59, 380.

5. See the comments of O. Plöger on this passage in *Das Buch Daniel* (Oütersloh: Mohn, 1965).

6. W. S. Towner, *Daniel* (Atlanta: Knox, 1984), on the passage.

7. C. Westermann, *Praise and Lament in the Psalms* (Atlanta/ Edinburgh: Knox/Clark, 1981), 171–72, 206.

8. N. W. Porteous, *Daniel* (London/Philadelphia: SCM/ Westminister, 1965; rev. ed., 1979), on the passage.

Chapter 6 The Powers of Heaven
1. K. Barth, *Church Dogmatics* iii, 3 (Edinburgh/New York: Clark/Scribner's, 1960), 460-63.
2. R. A. Anderson, *Signs and Wonders: A Commentary on the Book of Daniel* (Edinburgh/Grand Rapids: Handsel/Eerdmans, 1984), on the passage.
3. W. Wink, *Unmasking the Powers* (Philadelphia: Fortress, 1986), 89.

Chapter 7 Perspectives on History
1. "Spätisraelitische Geschichtsdenken am Beispiel des Buches Daniel," *Historische Zeitschrift* 193 (1961), 25-32.
2. So D. Flusser, "The four empires in the Fourth Sybil and in the Book of Daniel," *Israel Oriental Studies* 2 (1972), 166-68.
3. W. Lüthi, *The Church to Come* (London: Hodder, 1939) or the U.S. edition, *Daniel Speaks to the Church* (Minneapolis: Augsburg, 1947), on the passage.
4. S. J. DeVries, *The Achievements of Biblical Religion* (Lanham, Md./London: University Press of America, 1983), 342.

Chapter 9 The End
1. S. Niditch, *The Symbolic Vision in Biblical Tradition* (Chico, Calif.: Scholars, 1983), 209-15.
2. J. Calvin, *Commentaries on the Book of the Prophet Daniel*, 2 vols. (Edinburgh: CTS, 1852-53), on the passage.
3. P. R. Davies, *Daniel* (Sheffield: JSOT, 1985), 97.
4. See Chrysostom's commentary published in *Patrologia Graeca* 56 (1862), 193-246.
5. W. Dietrich, "Gott als König," ZTK 77 (1980), 251-68.

SELECT BIBLIOGRAPHY

Aukerman, D. *Darkening Valley*. New York: Seabury, 1981. (A book on the Bible and political issues, focusing on the nuclear threat; suggestive for issues raised by a book such as Daniel.)

Baldwin, J. G. *Daniel*. Leicester/Grand Rapids: IVP/Eerdmans, 1978. (The best conservative exegetical treatment.)

Calvin, J. *Commentaries on the Book of the Prophet Daniel*. 2 vols. Tr. T. Myers. Edinburgh: CTS, 1852-53 and often reprinted. (Calvin is always worth reading for his theological exposition.)

Collins, J. J. *Daniel*. Grand Rapids: Eerdmans, 1984. (A form-critical treatment by an acknowledged expert on Daniel.)

Davies, P. R. *Daniel*. Sheffield: JSOT, 1985. (A survey of current scholarly study.)

Goldingay, J. *Daniel*. Word Biblical Commentary, vol. 30. Dallas, Tex.: Word, 1989. (The detailed commentary which underlies the present work.)

Heaton, E. W. *The Book of Daniel*. London: SCM, 1956. (An older brief commentary still worth reading because of its independence and insight.)

Lacocque, A. *The Book of Daniel*. Tr. D. Pellauer. London/Atlanta: SPCK/Knox, 1979. (A more extensive independent exegetical commentary.)

Lüthi, W. *The Church to Come*. Tr. D. H. C. Read. London: Hodder and Stoughton, 1939. American ed., *Daniel Speaks to the Church*. Tr. J. M. Jensen. Minneapolis: Augsburg, 1947. (An exposition first written in the 1930s, a suggestive context for preaching on Daniel.)

Montgomery, J. A. *A Critical and Exegetical Commentary on the Book of Daniel*. Edinburgh/New York: Clark/Scribner's, 1927. (The classic critical commentary, still indispensable.)

Porteous, N. W. *Daniel*. London/Philadelphia: SCM/Westminster, 1965. Rev. ed., 1979. (A warm, brief, theological commentary.)

Russell, D. S. *Daniel: An Active Volcano*. Edinburgh/Philadelphia: St. Andrew/Westminster, 1989). The best brief exposition.

Towner, W. S. *Daniel*. Atlanta: Knox, 1984. (A more adventurous recent theological exposition.)

Wallace, R. S. *The Lord is King: The Message of Daniel*. Leicester/Downers Grove, Ill.: IVP, 1979. (A detailed exposition, moderately conservative.)

Wink, W. *Naming the Powers*. Philadelphia: Fortress, 1984.

———. *Unmasking the Powers*. Philadelphia: Fortress, 1986. (The first two parts of a three-part study of the way the Bible speaks of supernatural powers, such as Daniel often refers to.)

INDEX OF SCRIPTURES

Index of Scriptures